LIVING
WITH
BOOKS

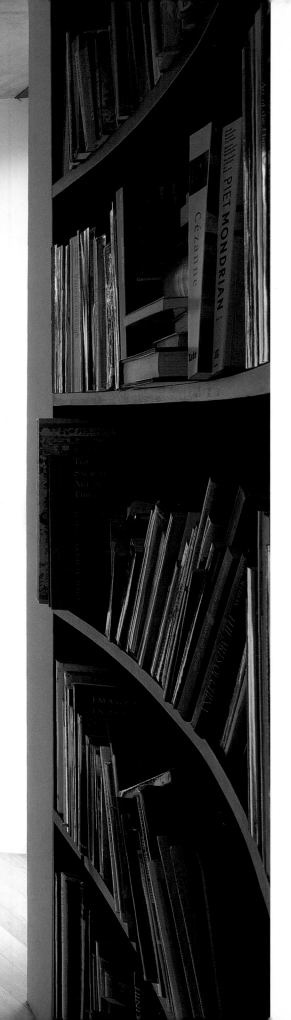

LIVING
WITH
BOOKS

ALAN POWERS

SOMA
san francisco

To Eleanor

LIVING WITH BOOKS
by Alan Powers

First published in 1999 by Mitchell Beazley,
an imprint of Octopus Publishing Group Ltd,
2-4 Heron Quays, London E14 4JB
North American hardcover edition published 1999,
North American softcover edition published 2002,
by SOMA Books, by arrangement with Mitchell Beazley.

SOMA Books is an imprint of Bay/SOMA Publishing, Inc.,
444 De Haro St., No. 130, San Francisco, CA 94107.

For the Mitchell Beazley edition:
Executive Editor **Alison Starling**
Executive Art Editor **Vivienne Brar**
Editor **Elisabeth Faber**
Designer **Martin Lovelock**
Production **Paul Hammond**
Picture Research **Jo Walton**
Index **Sue Farr**

Text and line artworks for pp.128–139 by Mark Ripley
Color illustrations for pp.128–139 by Amanda Patton

For the SOMA edition:
Publisher **James Connolly**
Art Director **Jeffrey O'Rourke**
Editorial Director **Clancy Drake**
North American Editor **Heather Garnos**
Production **Patrick David Barber**

Library of Congress cataloging-in-publication data
on file with the publisher

ISBN 1-57959-024-1 (hardcover)
ISBN 1-57959-073-X (softcover)
Printed in China
10 9 8 7 6 5 4 3 2

Distributed by Publishers Group West

CONTENTS

A book is an information resource. It contains a text that may be useful in different ways. The text can now come to us in different forms, electronically, on disk, or on an audio tape, so does the bound stack of paper have any special place left in the modern world? We may now have fully entered into an age where, for the first time in five hundred years, since the invention of printing with movable type, the book is no longer a primary means of communication. Yet it seems unlikely that the book will easily drop out of our lives, since it is not, after all, a neutral information resource like any other, but a cultural artifact with a variety of meanings accumulated over time.

What we normally understand by the word "book" is what the ancient world called a codex, which was created when sheets of parchment were folded up and cut to make pages. It was easily portable, and its popularity in the

Above A woodcut of a seventeenth-century printer's workshop. In the background, type is being made up into pages from typecases. The press is worked by two men, one to ink the pages with leather pads, the other to take sheets of paper on and off the press. They are printing four pages at a time on a single sheet, which will later be folded and bound.

Left In this medieval illustration, St. Augustine is depicted at work writing a book in his study. The book press behind him shows the books laid horizontally rather than shelved vertically. The doors enable these objects – precious treasures in the Middle Ages – to be locked away safely.

Below The early days of printing in Germany. Essentially, very little changed in printing processes until the nineteenth century. In spite of the simple technology, fine craftsmen could produce excellent results with metal type and handmade paper. Many printers also operated as publishers and editors, making important decisions to publish texts that changed the course of Western thinking.

Roman world came at the same time as the growth in private silent reading. The book could be said, therefore, to have two separate moments of birth, first as a completely handmade object, written by a scribe, and second, nearly 1,500 years later, with Johann Gutenberg's invention of printing in Germany in the 1450s. Until after World War II, printing remained almost entirely within the technical limits of Gutenberg's method of taking an impression from a raised surface, although presses became much faster during the nineteenth century with steam power, and paper became cheaper, though normally of much poorer quality than before. The next important change in technology was the replacement of metal type by photocomposition and lithographic printing during the 1960s, which made books even easier to produce and more widely available.

"There is in the life of a collector a dialectical tension between the poles of disorder and order," wrote the nomadic scholar Walter Benjamin in the 1930s, describing the unpacking of his library. He understood how books have a symbolic meaning that is not dependent on their usefulness, although being useful gives them a special priority over other possessions. To know that any book is, in theory, obtainable in a good library, is no substitute for having your own copy, with its particular history and associations. Benjamin describes the pleasure of the chase that lies behind the most satisfying book purchases: "one of the finest memories of a collector is the moment when he rescued a book to which he might never have given a thought, much less a wishful look, because he found it lonely and abandoned on the market place and bought it to give it its freedom – the way the prince bought a beautiful slave girl in *The Arabian Nights*. To a book collector, you see, the true freedom of all books is somewhere on his shelves."

It is this almost human quality in books that contributes to the pleasure of owning them. They deserve a proper setting and can give more pleasure when housed thoughtfully and appropriately. There needs to be a balance between the character of the house, the character of the owner, and the type of books that live there. It is impossible to imagine all the different ways in which books can contribute to houses, and vice-versa.

Below The workroom of the composer Johannes Brahms. The simple wooden shelves across the end of the room, blocking off a doorway, have a remarkably modern character, partly because of their lack of ornament, and partly in their slightly makeshift appearance.

Above A print published in 1813 by Rudolph Ackermann showing a "circulating library," where books were lent to subscribers. Books were by now more widely available and the spread of knowledge accelerated social changes, culminating in the development of free public libraries in the late nineteenth century.

Left In this mid-nineteenth century bourgeois German interior, the plain room, with its functional bookshelves, indicates that the sitter is a serious scholar. By the time this was painted, owning a study full of books was no longer solely a privilege of the very rich.

A substantial collection of books needs a special room to house it. The library of a private house usually doubles as a study, but can have other uses. The earliest libraries, dating from the sixteenth century, were not primarily social rooms, but by the late eighteenth century, as books became more widely available, more fully illustrated and less serious in content, a change was taking place, turning the library into a comfortable room in which all members of the household might gather informally. The new type of library can be seen to perfection at Kenwood House, on London's Hampstead Heath. Designed by Robert Adam in 1767, the room contains built-in bookshelves, but the greater part of the wall surface is covered with mirrors. Gilded sofas and chairs and a ceiling decorated with allegorical paintings complete the effect. By 1838, J. C. Loudon, the popular writer on decoration, could claim that "in the present day, no villa, or suburban residence, having more than two sitting rooms, can be considered complete without a library."

Opposite This working library in a Milan penthouse elegantly brings together several different forms of book storage and display. The central library table, which includes flat file drawers, has cantilevered shelves at either end.

Below The roof space in this studiolike library is cleverly used to house a built-in gallery, which extends outwards to accommodate an inviting table and chair. This is a welcoming, lived-in room, with its comfortable furniture and pictures, and natural light streaming in through the skylight.

Libraries in houses today are comfortable, welcoming rooms, sometimes more like the cabinets and studies of the Renaissance. They represent the extension of a personal world, whether their purpose is the active research of the scholar, the pride of possession of the collector, or the random acquisitiveness of the curious mind. Books in these situations need to be visible, but they do not have to march along the shelves with the orderliness of a professional cataloger's numbering system. The standard sizes of modern books are certainly an advantage to the designer of libraries, as the natural and logical way of arranging them is in diminishing order of size, from floor to ceiling. This produces a classical correctness of proportion in the spacing of the shelves, which is not unlike the relationship between the different sizes of window in the façade of a Georgian house.

Library shelving frequently follows the pattern of what was originally a movable bookcase, called in French *à deux corps*, with a glass- or lattice-fronted upper cabinet and cupboards below up to dado height. The lower section is the equivalent of the full pedestal of a classical column, with a little shelf before the main section of shelving begins, corresponding to the base of the column and its shaft. The upper level is

Above The library in the house of twentieth-century Swedish sculptor Carl Milles. The bookcases have simplified classical details, which are reproduced in the furniture. The very wide shelves in the center section of the built-in bookcase would normally be considered visually unsatisfactory, but here their horizontal emphasis creates a feeling of calm, diverting attention from the walls and on to the room itself. The warm grays, typical of the Swedish neoclassical style, make for an interior that is both light and restful.

Left This unconventional modern treatment gives character to a confined space. The cupboard, with its "sleeping eye" door handles, resembles a cubist face; its offbeat design is reinforced by the skewed rug. Although this library does not have the advantage of natural light, the white painted floor helps to maximize light filtering in from the outer room. The reading light itself is suspended low over the table and covered with a wide, opaque shade to protect the reader's eyes.

completed with a continuous band in the form of a cornice or frieze. Sometimes these classical allusions are spelled out with actual columns and capitals; more often they are implied in the sense of ascending hierarchy and in the well-proportioned design, which makes the bookcase convenient to use as well as beautiful to look at.

The success or failure of the design of a library will probably depend not on the bookshelves or cases as such, but on the quality of light. There are certain functional demands, of course, either by day or by night, but the space itself is also controlled by light. Careful consideration needs to be given to the relationship between the position in which the reader is to sit and the rest of the room. Reading is not just an activity of the mind, but of the whole body, and natural light offers the most satisfying ambience, shifting and varying as it does. The new British Library in London incorporates the latest technology but has been designed so that the reading spaces are naturally lit. At home, natural light should also be used whenever possible. Care should be taken that other light sources, including reflections, do not cause accidental glare. At night, lights for reading should not be too high up or too bright.

Above A gallerylike minimalist interior in the home of a London art dealer. The solid wood bookshelves are important in giving scale and definition to a room in which there is little else for the eye to rest on. In this open-plan space, the shelves also serve to divide the library and living areas.

Library furniture does not have to be dark, and the examples illustrated here are striking in their use of light-colored natural timber or paint. Many libraries in both modern and period homes interrupt the regular ranks of shelves with a doorway, or some other opening, giving a sense of space beyond, rather than forming a cocoon. The late-Victorian popularizer of the Aesthetic movement, Mrs. Haweis, wrote that, "in pale blue, white or green, varnished and thoroughly dried before the books are put in, bookshelves may be made a real addition in beauty…niches may be lined with Japanese gilt papers, and the doors painted with flowers, insects, shells, creatures[?] or more ambitious subjects…I prefer the furniture of a study or a library a little gay in colour, because a mass of books, even gilt-backed, unrelieved, always tells dark and heavy."

Eighteenth- and nineteenth-century architects built bookshelves into the thickness of the wall, with a timber architrave flush to the line of the plaster, with the result that the cubic character of the interior space was maintained. The construction of the bookshelves in relation to the room is an important consideration when planning the design of a library from scratch. Modern building methods seldom give any depth of wall to play with, so it will usually be necessary to build the library as a shell inside a room. It is part of the designer's skill to remodel the existing space to good effect, and to prevent it from feeling either too crowded or too formal, or from having too great a vertical emphasis.

Opposite Books tend not to curve, but here the library creates a sense of enclosure, with views above and beyond, which is valuable in defining the space in an open-plan apartment.

Above A grid of compartments turns these shelves into an architectural object in themselves. Subtle variations in the sizes of the compartments add interest to the simple basic form.

Left Strong color provides a theme for this landing space, which also shows the aesthetic value of allowing a shelving unit to occupy a whole wall.

Overleaf In this library, the gallery, stair rail, and half-columns demarcating the major bays are all unifying devices, helping to organize a large wall of books and creating a classical hierarchy of forms. Attractive architectural features, galleries also serve a practical purpose – without the books, there would be no rationale for extending upwards.

THE DECORATIVE LIBRARY

A "neo-traditional" library has become a common feature in many homes, possibly formed in the back room on the main floor of a townhouse, or in a section of an open-plan apartment. Such a library will typically have painted or stained timber shelves. Below dado height, there may be cupboards, then a series of shelves of convenient height, topped off by a cornice. The cupboards may conceal rather un-bookish interests, being particularly well adapted to concealing such evidence of modern technology as the television, VCR, or stereo. Racks can also be built in for storing compact discs. The space above the bookcase is much prized for the display of what George Smith, in his *Cabinet-Maker and Upholsterer's Guide* of 1826, described as "antique vases or pieces of curious ornamental china."

Edith Wharton and Ogden Codman, authors of *The Decoration of Houses* (1902), had evidently seen enough libraries designed on this principle to desire an alternative. The French libraries of the eighteenth century were their standard of perfection. "In rooms of any importance," they wrote, "the French architect always preferred to build his book-shelves into niches formed in the thickness of the wall, thus utilising the books as part of his scheme of decoration…To adorn the walls of a library, and then conceal their ornamentation by expensive bookcases, is a waste, or rather a misapplication, of effects – always a sin against aesthetic principles."

Right A certain formality of design is never out of place in a library, particularly when counterpointed by unexpected details like these copper light fittings, the model pheasant, and the fine Windsor chair. The windows at upper level are an essential source of natural light, while also giving the effect of a "room within a room."

Above Libraries in older houses often share the scrubbed, no-frills quality of modern interiors. Here a Victorian patent fireproof ceiling sets the tone for a room where "what you see is what you get," although the hanging oil lamp appears to be more decorative than functional.

Left Books tend to be warm colored and to contrast well with strong, cool shades, such as the sea green of these bookshelves. The contrast extends to the floor tiles and to the library steps, in a modern design that looks reassuringly sturdy. The resulting ensemble uses traditional elements but updates them. The door handles and reeded shelf moldings add the barest of decorative touches.

Books need to be spread around in a library, not just confined to shelves, and horizontal surfaces are required for new arrivals, or perhaps for the display of particularly attractive covers or bindings. Magazines and newspapers are most readily found if lying flat. Moreover, it is often preferable to read at a table rather than in an armchair, to concentrate the mind, and also to keep several books open at once when cross-referencing or making notes. Many fine-art books published today are too large and heavy to be held easily on the lap, let alone to be read in bed, and so a well-lit table with an upright but comfortable chair is desirable. The Elizabethans had specially embroidered pillows on which to place books, which would have helped to protect the bindings; this custom might usefully be revived by collectors of antiquarian books.

Above This apparently austere seventeenth-century research library manages to make room for a few frivolities, mainly in the form of painted beams. The free-standing bookcases would properly be described as book presses. The green-painted wooden grilles are bold enough to act as a decorative feature in their own right.

Right Where a ceiling is particularly high, bookshelves can be carried upwards, to be reached by ladders. Here, in a literal example of loft living, the shelves reproduce the shape of the roof, while the sliding ladder gives access to all compartments. Books on high shelves have the same attraction as the apple on the top of the tree, demanding a perilous journey aloft.

Left The library and study of Harry Gullichsen at the Villa Mairea, in Finland, was designed by Alvar Aalto in 1939 as part of his redecoration of the house. It is one of the most attractive rooms of the interwar period.

Putnam County Library

EXPLORING BOOKSTORES

The pleasure of owning books begins in a bookstore. Each one has a character of its own, which helps to make books different from other commodities. Second-hand bookstores have the most individual stock and are usually run by knowledgeable people with a real love for books. There is a real thrill of the chase in finding something special or rare. New books can also be sold in distinctive surroundings, whether in a small individual shop, or in a branch of one of the many retailing chains.

A wise bookstore owner will encourage customers to take plenty of time, even if they seem to be using the shop more as a library. Sofas and chairs are becoming more common, and stores often provide comfortable corners in which people can lose themselves for a while. Children's books have specially designed areas with low-level shelves and fun furniture, so that the bookstore habit is learned young. Many larger bookstores are open throughout the week until late at night, offering an almost irresistible temptation to the city dweller.

Above Apparent disorder rules this second-hand bookstore, but the sun slants in benignly. No doubt the proprietor knows exactly what is in the shop and where to find it. Not knowing what you will come across next is part of the fun of browsing, however.

Left The bookstore in the Tate Gallery, Liverpool, designed by Michael Wilford and Associates, is an attractive space converted from an old warehouse. The books laid out on the tables and stands invite the visitor to dip in, and also reflect the trend in domestic interiors for displaying art books on tables.

Right The bookstore as home away from home, with soft furnishings, pictures, and flowers. In spite of the growth of mail-order bookselling, and competition from other kinds of media for home entertainment, bookstores are enjoying a late twentieth-century renaissance.

Left London's most elegant small bookstore, Heywood Hill in Curzon Street, was established in the 1930s. It not only sells books, but is a place for the exchange of literary and social gossip, where the staff members know their customers' likes and dislikes. New and old books are sold side by side, an ideal arrangement offering the widest range of knowledge and entertainment.

In a home, the difference between an office and a library may be hard to define. A library is often the place where activities such as reading, writing, or drawing are carried out, whether they are regarded as leisure pursuits or professional employment. Yet there is a type of room (or part of a room) that can be seen immediately as an "office" where "work" takes place. The difference is a subtle one, indicated perhaps by the greater conspicuousness of the computer, fax machine, or telephone. The distinction between home library and office is made partly for the benefit of the user, to encourage the right frame of mind for working, when other distractions might offer themselves. Twenty years ago, only a small number of freelancers regularly used the home as a place of work. Now, a series of social and technological changes has made working at home not only commonplace, but often unavoidable. Work patterns have shifted toward greater flexibility, particularly for women. Many offices are much smaller than they used to be, and do not provide a permanent base, even for a full-time job. Technology makes it possible to do without secretaries and receptionists and to be a one-person office, with computer, fax, internet connection, and answering machine, all taking up progressively less space as the equipment is miniaturized. While the current fashion in office design and management is for ever more openness of plan, the home office has also become a haven of privacy and individuality.

Left An architect's book-lined workspace. The drawing board stands on a gateleg dining table and the telephone is discreetly housed among the books. Seating is provided by a "balloon-back" dining chair, a typical nineteenth-century design. This home office shows how the trappings of modern working life can be made to fit seamlessly into a period home. It succeeds in conveying the idea of home, but is also austere enough to stimulate work.

Left This office, which is housed in a spare bedroom, has a trestle table for a desk. The shelving system is an ingenious design that can be taken down and reassembled should the worker's requirements change. The uprights are braced between floor and ceiling, supporting cantilever brackets inserted into the open slots, which give the shelves a chunky look that recalls the Constructivist designs associated with craftsmen in post-revolutionary Russia. These shelves do not need to be fixed to the wall and could easily be moved from one house to another.

Above This corner beside a blocked-off chimney breast could have been a wasted space but has instead been used for storing books and files. The simple design of the shelves, the metal finish of the desk and the angled lamp all suggest industriousness and efficiency.

Right After years of hard treatment, an old kitchen table has been given a new lease on life as a spacious desk in a home office. Note the pull-up blind, which shades the table without darkening the room.

Above In this intimate home office, modern shelving is fitted into the structure of an old house. The workspace has been carefully planned, with plenty of natural light and books close at hand.

Left The office as eagle's nest: how to work in the whole space of the house while keeping demarcation lines clear. This elegant architectural solution also contrasts old floorboards with smooth new materials.

A PERSONALIZED WORKSPACE

While, to some extent, a home office needs to foster a serious attitude toward work, it can also be a place with a strong sense of individual style. Books that are used regularly for work become essential companions. Certain kinds of creative work require instant access to a range of books, be they reference books or other extensions of the owner's mental furniture. Books specific to particular subjects also tend to project their own aura. This is the home office as library, the kind of cell-like room used by nineteenth-century writers to shut themselves off from the world. Examples include Thomas Carlyle's attic on Cheyne Row, Chelsea, or Marcel Proust's cork-lined room in Paris.

Such a room is different, however, from a place where the telephone rings, where the outside world comes into the home. This second type of home office is more like the Victorian man's "business room," part of the "masculine" space of the house, which is deliberately coded through its decoration to

differ from the "feminine" spaces. To describe such areas in this way no longer, of course, implies an actual gender difference. Most people, men and women, want some distinction between different kinds of rooms, if only to provide variety of mood.

In any room in which books play a conspicuous part, the style language will be assembled from diverse elements. The presence of books certainly implies shelves, which are likely to be less ornamental in an office than in a library. Here, if anywhere, prefabricated shelving systems will come into their own. The busy office worker will find them quick and convenient to set up, and to rearrange if necessary. These systems are also designed to meet many different storage requirements. There is a range of ready-made shelving to suit all budgets, and even the cheapest can look very presentable, although shelves made of fiberboard rather than timber have a tendency to sag under heavy weights.

At the height of the Art Deco movement in the 1920s, the architect Le Corbusier held up standard office furniture as the model for all modern furniture, rather than pieces using traditional joinery and upholstery skills. The aesthetic of the workplace was adopted throughout the home by a small band of important modernist designers, resulting in such work as the Eames storage unit system, designed by Charles and Ray Eames in 1950, which seemed to predict the merging of work and home some forty years before it really began to happen.

Above Cupboards are essential to minimalist living. These give character to a small home workspace and gain greatly from being lifted off the ground. A rail for a ladder runs across the shelves, having a decorative as well as a functional purpose, in tune with the wire-legged table by André Dubreuil.

Right In this open workspace, the looped light cord gives character to what is otherwise a sparsely decorated interior, inverting the curve at the top of the window. The natural flooring contrasts with the metal structure of the office table. For a close-up of the bookshelf in this room, see pp. 36–7.

Left An example of truly minimal living: a filing cabinet hollowed out of a fireplace and bookshelves concealed behind cupboard doors. The glass-topped table offers a large work surface without detracting from the light, airy feel of the room. This is the home equivalent of the paperless office, carefully thought through and detailed.

Overleaf Too many books can create a cluttered, disorganized impression in an office, but here the single shelf has been used creatively, with the insertion of black-and-white photographs of Indian sculptures. The well-worn bindings of the older books correspond to the weathered stone in the photographs.

Above Conversions of old buildings have never been more popular, and this light-filled office makes good use of the original structure. The workspace extends upwards above the bare wooden beams, with access provided by a white ladder. The shelves are simple box units that float above the floor.

Right The space beneath the gallery defines the work area in a living room where office equipment is stored side by side with evidence of more recreational pursuits. The three glass-fronted cabinets add depth and variety to what would otherwise be a stark arrangement of shelving and storage units.

WORKING AND LIVING

Successful home offices can be formed within the space of a larger, more sociable room, preventing the worker from becoming isolated. Harry Gullichsen's library at the Villa Mairea (see p. 22) was designed in this way and was used both for his own work and for meetings. The winding wall that Alvar Aalto designed to separate the library from the larger workspace creates an agreeable sense of enclosure while also reminding those outside of the important work going on within. Yet this sort of division does not need to be so complete. If the ceiling is high enough, the same effect can be achieved by changing the floor level and working perched up above the main room. An alternative is to build an enclosure with partitions at shoulder height, so that when the worker sits down, there is no visual distraction from beyond. When it is wide enough on top, a partition of this type also makes a good surface for shelves and storage. Ideally, it should not consist of a four-square box, but should have a rounded form to enable it to fit more gracefully into the outer space.

Below The roof terrace makes a pleasant view for anyone working under the sloping ceiling in this top-floor office. The desk is narrow enough not to block the French windows that give access to the terrace. The use of the same wall covering on the ceiling and cupboard doors under the shelves is an old trick, helping to tie all the elements together.

A home office may need to be used for other functions, doubling as a dining room, for example. There is much to be said, therefore, for the current trend toward minimalism, which entails first a rigorous selection of items, and then a search for the best ways to keep them out of view. It may be necessary to use cupboards, the doors of which can become decorative features in their own right through the use of color and surface treatment. Such doors may open in the usual way, but space-saving sliding doors are also worth considering where the room is wide enough to take them. The later Victorians were very keen on curtains as a means of concealing anything that did not meet with their approval, but contemporary interiors seem often to banish textiles altogether. Opportunities should be found to use all the available volume in the home office, even down to odd spaces and openings in the thickness of the wall, such as old fireplaces. In rooms with a dual function, the ephemera of the day's work can be put quickly and efficiently out of sight outside office hours, using storage units on wheels, or even an armoire.

Opposite In this elegant yet simple and functional office, with its strong color notes, red doors fly open, revealing…something quite ordinary. The expectations raised and subtly undermined by this ingenious shelving unit are the basis for a designer's visual joke.

Left The bookshelf becomes desk becomes drawing table, and its clear surface is one element in a disappearing act that is repeated in the Plexiglas base of the stool. The sides of the shelves are raised above the work surface, creating a "room within a room."

Left A no-frills office in a large square room, which is elegant enough not to be dominated by the floor-to-ceiling bookshelves. A well-thought-out home office such as this provides a balance of stimulus and calm, achieved through careful planning of the workspace and attention to lighting. The worker's chair has been placed in order to give a good view of the door, so that visitors can be seen coming and, if necessary, warned off.

Left This home office places the emphasis on "office" rather than "home," perhaps, but it remains a light and cheerful room, with plenty of structural and design features to carry the eye into the spaces. The sliding white doors behind the desk could be used for slide projection and help to balance the impact of so many layers of books.

Most people who work in a home office find it preferable to occupy the space in the middle of the room, where they are able to look around them, than to sit crowded against a wall or in a corner. An ordinary table will serve as a desk, as designers seem not to offer many alternatives. The home worker will probably need storage for documents and files as well as books, some of which may be in open-top cardboard cartons. These workaday units can be personalized by the use of color coding, bold lettering, or other functional kinds of decoration. Filing cabinets may also be a necessity. Two-drawer cabinets can double as a convenient work surface, with shelves above. Four-drawer cabinets look best in groups of three or more. They are likely to make a prominent feature in any room, and manufacturers seldom supply them in attractive colors, but they are easy to paint, and can be further cheered up by the use of two-color paint schemes. Personal computers make it possible to keep fewer documents in hard-copy form, helping to reduce the need for filing cabinets and maximize limited working space. The "work station" will remain the central focus of most offices, at least until computers and other equipment become so "virtual" as to be invisible.

TROMPE L'ŒIL

FAKES &

As a subject for pure decoration, books offer many opportunities. Long before the Surrealist movement, designers and decorators had discovered the potential of playing with trompe l'œil books, making false doors in bookcases covered with artificial book spines, and book-shaped objects. In the 1820s the essayist Charles Lamb said "I can read anything which I call a *book*" but not "Draught Boards bound and lettered at the back" to look like books. In the 1920s and 1930s, there was a fashion for making cigarette boxes from old books hollowed out – damaging books as well as health. The tradition of deception was continued in the postwar period by designer-decorators such as Piero Fornasetti in Italy, who produced bookcases and cabinets with imitation books, as well as screens and fabrics with similar motifs.

This kind of deceit may have a practical purpose of concealing something that would look out of place among other books, or it may just take the idea of books as something to play with. Our eyes are so used to seeing shelves of books as a background that it comes as a pleasant surprise to discover that what we see is not what we get. In these cases, books lose their practical function and become entirely decorative.

Above In the library of the composer George Gershwin, most of the musical scores on this shelf are real, but some of them are actually false spines painted onto a hi-fi speaker, a skilled and ingenious deception.

Above and Right Two pieces by Fornasetti that use trompe l'oeil books in different ways. The side table takes them out of context, while the cabinet shows them in their "proper" place, but with a mysterious curtained view.

Left A superb wallpaper
in imitation of books by
Brunschwig & Fils. While many
trompe l'œil books are rather
dull in themselves, these are
particularly decorative and
appealing, showing, incidentally,
how a shelf of books might be
more attractive than its usually
slightly dull self. Some of these
wallpaper books seem to be
bound in (imitation) wallpaper.
Would it be too confusing to
use pieces of this wallpaper to
cover real books?

Right A modern version of an
old device, where doors in a
library are disguised by false
book fronts. This is particularly
subtle because the "books" are
behind glass, so it is less easy to
work out what they are.

HALLWAYS AND ODD SPACES

The key indicator of any household's attitude toward books is not whether one room has been specially allocated for the purpose of housing them, serving as a library or study. Such an arrangement requires no particular affinity for books. In a truly bookish house, by comparison, there are no parts that do *not* contain books, and it is possible to judge the level of devotion (or bibliomania) by the ingenuity with which odd spaces are adapted to the purpose. This does not mean that every room or passageway ought to resemble a library. Books can appear in many different guises and make a contribution to any space if they are introduced with a conscious sense of design. Mixing books with other objects, practical or decorative, is one of the most creative and productive ways of living with them in the home. Books can be used as decoration and as a means of creating atmosphere, but perhaps more importantly, they also have the ability to influence the structure of the space around them. Another advantage to storing books throughout the home is that it encourages the reading habit by combining this with other forms of domestic activity.

Right Winding steps reveal books ascending to the light, all neatly boxed into the thickness of the wall, with shelves of matching wood. The relationship between shelving and stairs, emphasized by inspired use of lighting, perfectly demonstrates how what might otherwise be thought of as a "dead" space can be opened up to provide extra storage while also being made more pleasing visually.

Below In a house of enthusiasms, books take their place alongside majestic toy trains and antique cameras. This display ingeniously capitalizes on the change in floor level and the potential of the space to allow for different thicknesses of shelf. Some of the boxlike shelves appear to project into space.

STAIRS AND LANDINGS

To fill an entire house with books, absent-minded scholars will start by using the floor, creating skyscrapers of books which must on no account be disturbed because they represent research in progress. The stairs are also useful, since there is about a foot on either side of each tread that is surplus to the minimum requirement for walking up and down, and this space makes a valuable filing system. It is possible to live under these conditions, but hard for those who are not like-minded to share such a dwelling. However, a large collection of books can be more gracefully accommodated through the use of ingenious design solutions that still leave room for the house to function normally. An added bonus is that some of the lost space in the house, in hallways and corridors, on staircases and landings, is brought into use and becomes more attractive as a result. There are even certain kinds of books that seem to belong in these intermediate positions – maps and guidebooks, perhaps, which can be picked up on the run or in meditative moments of wanderlust.

Opposite In the cavernous space of this uncompromisingly modernist house, which belongs to a London architect, a wall of books becomes an important element in creating a transitional space between the lower and upper floors. Viewed from below, floating way overhead, these books create an aura of unattainable desire.

Left Professional librarians would probably not recommend this storage system. It hinders efficient retrieval and may result in damage to the books or even injury to the reader. Designers, on the other hand, are likely to view this sort of arrangement more favorably, since it looks sensational and makes maximum use of the space.

Modern architecture was based in part on the idea of open space rather than closed rooms. For example, in villas designed by Le Corbusier in Paris in the 1920s, there were hardly any rooms as such, only circulation spaces with sitting places. (Ironically, it is not in new buildings but in the conversion of old ones that architects nowadays chiefly get the chance to realize this part of the modernist philosophy.) When books are housed in the transit zones of a house, modernist or otherwise, it is important to follow this dictum and not allow the books to take over completely.

The flow of space is one of the pleasures of a house, and it requires tact to manage it effectively. The solutions illustrated here to the problem of housing books in unconventional spaces show how it is possible to provide stopping-off places without unduly interrupting the journey. Surprise has long been recognized as a major factor in successful design, and bookshelves offer many opportunities for inventive and original ideas that give the impression not that a house has too many books, but that it is a place where delightful novelty can be encountered at every turn.

Above Books on the balcony: this portion of an open-plan space is given a function of its own and also made habitable by the simple, continuous runs of books and the congenial double recliner. Here, two people could perhaps read one book together, like Abélard and Héloïse in medieval Paris.

Left This boldly defined flight of steps helps to solve the problem of how to gain access to the higher shelves, and provides an additional means of displaying books. Above all, it turns an otherwise conventional space into a unique and memorable one, illustrating the importance of achieving the correct proportions in order to create a successful whole.

Left This house in Islington, north London, designed by the architects Future Systems, was constructed in 1994 and was instantly famous. A radical reworking of a London site, it provides the maximum run of vertical shelving, appropriately using a lightweight metal system.

INTRICATE SPACES

The way that books are displayed in a living space is an important consideration for any designer. Seeing a group of books stimulates a desire to reach out for them, and a little reading space beside them, even without a chair, can make part of a room feel instantly alluring. This is the attraction of window seats, where one can step outside the flow of the room. Charlotte Brontë describes her lonely ten-year-old heroine reading Bewick's *History of British Birds* in this manner in the opening chapter of *Jane Eyre*: "I mounted up into the window seat: gathering up my feet, I sat cross-legged, like a Turk; and, having drawn the red moreen curtains nearly closed, I was shrined in double retirement."

Placing shelves on different floor levels can turn getting hold of a book into a little journey, while a circuitous approach route can be constructed on the principles of garden design, where you can see something in the distance, and lose it before finding it again. These devices can be used in a small space to make it appear larger. With a twist of the unexpected, books can be inserted quite elegantly into places where they might not normally be found.

Much can be achieved by going against the usual expectations of book shelving and making shelves play a positive part in the design of space, whether by projecting at right angles from the wall, taking the form of a shallow curve, or appearing as an independent object in an interior. The linear character of shelves counteracts the inevitable tendency of books that are often in use to look random and disarranged.

Right In the London home of the artist Anish Kapoor, a built-in shelf unit comes into view as you mount the stairs. The simple glass balustrade gives the maximum degree of transparency while also introducing a veiled effect. The light beyond the bookshelves adds to the sense of mystery, and the low book rest seems to be an invitation to read.

Right Artist Peter Blake's attic studio has a section of book shelving subtly inserted in the corner and shaded from direct light. With the dark posts rising from the stairs, a transitional space is created on the way into the studio, where one might pause to scan the shelves or sit to read on the step formed by the sill of the upper door.

Left An inspired solution to the problem of housing magazines in the hallway of a Milan apartment. There would hardly be room to project the shelves out into the space in the normal way, but as designed, they offer a wide passageway, convenient access to the magazines, and an intriguing effect of floating planes of blond wood to give structure to the space.

Previous page In a study area created under the eaves of a colonial-style house, unpainted bookshelves fit neatly around the narrow window. The shelves complement the bare wooden rafters, crossbeams, and balustrade and seem to form an integral part of the structure.

Far right The vertical tongue-and-groove paneling covering the walls makes a tall, narrow shelving arrangement seem entirely natural here. Arranging books horizontally has the advantage that where the book titles run down the spine, they can be read without rotating the head 90 degrees.

Above Maximum simplicity, maximum style. The shelves are slotted together and screwed top and bottom to the wall. Vertical books in this position would spoil the effect, but these closely spaced horizontal shelves make an attractive contribution to the area between kitchen and stairs.

Right The success of these shelves is due to the careful chasing into the wall plaster and the strong color contrast with the walls. The curves are reminiscent of the fins on an Art Deco building and there is a nice sense of proportion in the overall design. Too many books would spoil the line of these shelves.

Books can get in the way, so there is nothing wrong with putting them somewhere where they are difficult to get at, provided that the difficulty does not amount to total impossibility. Where there are small children in the house, this can even be a sensible precaution. High-up shelves help to soften the junction between wall and ceiling and make a room more cavelike and enclosing. The voids above staircases are another invitation to books. In reality, most collections contain books that are old friends but do not need to be visited very often. These can be placed somewhere within view but not necessarily immediately at hand. The more you build castles in the air with books, the more interesting that part of the house becomes.

Above In a penthouse high above the city, light and space seem to have come indoors. The books can be reached from the balcony, yet still appear to be floating in the middle distance.

Right These shelves in the "Whisky Barrel" house at Findhorn, an ecological community in Scotland, contribute to the homey atmosphere. The end of the shelves is organically shaped, making an architectural statement in keeping with the whole house.

Right The glassed-in enclosure, reached by a ladder that could have been salvaged from a ship, transforms this little book loft into a highly desirable space. The structure also makes clever use of a high-ceilinged transitional area, creating a welcoming and intimate atmosphere before the main living area is reached.

Transitional spaces are made more eventful if there are defined thresholds that need to be crossed on the journey. While modern architecture has gained freedom of space, it has lost the sense of a graduated journey that more traditional houses tend to create. These intervals modulate light and shade, stimulating the mind and making the space seem larger than it might otherwise appear. Perhaps, as some landscape theorists have suggested, our desire to be protected but to be able to see around us derives from the savannah country in which the human race is supposed to have originated, with trees growing at intervals in open land, affording protection from the direct sun and a good view of anything approaching.

The clever designer will manage to create the same sense of openness and enclosure at the same time by adjusting the dimensions and the lighting in the space, perhaps narrowing the sides, or lowering the headroom, or both. In either case, the opportunity arises for colonizing the newly created space with books, providing incident and humanizing the scale. When storing books in a transitional area, a short shelf is in many ways preferable to a long one, making it easier to locate a book while on the move and preventing books from falling over when several are removed from the shelf at the same time.

Left The keystone over the center of this doorway makes a powerful architectural statement that is carried through in the careful finishing of the baseboards and moldings, suggesting a mannerist door within a door, while providing a delightfully tantalizing glimpse of the dining room beyond. All this, and bookshelf space too!

Above Small windows are always an attractive feature, but even more so when they are set in deep recesses to filter the light. Here, the depth of the existing wall has been subtly enhanced by the simple bookshelves. Whether by accident or design, the old books match the textured quality of the plaster around the window.

Right This series of overhead shelves, each with its recessed lights, turns a potentially awkward hallway into a mysterious but also practical space. The library steps double as a telephone stool, but would be essential for access to the books. Placed out of reach in this way, books invariably seem much more interesting than before.

VISUAL HARMONY

The fewer the books in any given space, the more planning is needed to ensure that they do not look like an afterthought or a mistake. Shelving can seem merely expedient, or it can appear as a deliberate element of a larger design. Visual continuity is important, so that the eye is not jerked from one thing to another, and this implies the use of extended horizontal or vertical lines.

If the shelving is altering the surface of the wall, it needs to look as if it knows what it is doing, which again suggests that a broad treatment will be best. Within the shelving itself, the thickness of the edge profile is dictated not only by a minimum strength requirement but by a sense of how the whole shelf unit will look when seen from a distance. These fine calculations are the stuff of architecture and are beyond rule of thumb or rationalization. In rejecting ornament and decoration in favor of purity of line based on correct proportion, modern designers have deliberately set themselves this harder task of adjusting a few fundamentals to make a satisfying relationship.

Below A simple run of boxlike shelving attached to a wall fulfills a similar but more productive function to that of the dado or chair rail in traditional paneled rooms. This handy ledge is also at the right height for plants.

Right Stopping this shelf unit short of the corner makes all the difference to its contribution to the character of the room. It reads as a self-contained object in space, an effect that is enhanced by leaving one bay clear of books.

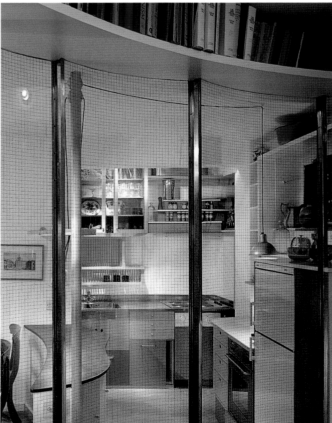

Opposite It is not easy to put bookshelves on a curve, but these shelves function as part of a broader architectural effect in the home of British architect Bill Dunster. They are painted in a warm color that goes well with the floor tiles and with the exposed brick and mortar in the screen of glass bricks.

Left Curves are important in this compact kitchen and dining area. The books overhead, combined with the glass screens, help to achieve the transition between two separate parts of an open-plan space.

Above These vaults make exciting enclosures off a larger shared space. The grid of bright red shelving brings together the diversity of books and toys to suggest order without formality. The way in which shelves occupy and project into a space is an important consideration when creating a successful interior, and these structures have the correct sense of scale, filling the whole of the far wall and helping to define the shape of the space.

hallways and odd spaces **67**

DESIGNER SOLUTIONS

It takes a lot of individual thought to find a new way of designing bookshelves, since the normal forms are so widely accepted, and in most cases so competent. Design in the late twentieth century is evolving largely in terms of lateral thinking, moving ideas from one area to another. This is not primarily motivated by a desire to improve the functional aspects of things. Instead it offers new ways of understanding the potential meanings of the objects encountered in daily life. This can have a refreshing effect in a world where so many things are standardized. From the success of many apparently "useless" products, it is clear that people buy things not just to serve their wants and needs, but to avoid boredom and monotony.

In the 1930s, the Isokon "Donkey" (illustrated below) made a beautiful match of material and manufacture with function and symbolized the aspiration to enjoy good things, such as inexpensive paperbacks, at prices that everyone could afford. It was relaunched after 1945 in a new version by Egon Riss with a flat top on which a drink could be placed, a practical advantage although probably an aesthetic loss.

Design today is no longer always so utopian – special objects like the "Donkey" seldom enter the mass market – but Ron Arad's "Bookworm" (see p. 79) is one novel variant on the bookshelf that has become such a cult icon that there is an entire book about it. As these pages show, young designers are still finding new and interesting ways to meet the challenge of book storage.

Right The "Donkey," designed in 1939 by Egon Riss for the British manufacturer Isokon, used the technique of bending plywood to create a new version of the traditional type of newspaper or magazine rack called a Canterbury. This design was ideally proportioned for the Penguin paperback series, launched in Britain in 1936, and was promoted on the back covers of their books. The "Donkey" on the right is shown loaded with Penguins.

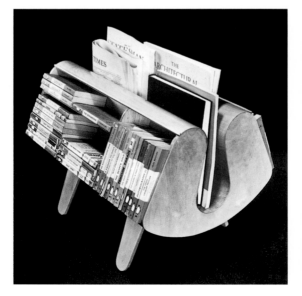

Left A storage system (1998) by London-based designer Gitta Gschwendtner. When empty, the boxes make a grid pattern on the wall, but each one is mounted on a hidden spring, and drops down when something is placed inside it. The boxes lean to the right or left depending on which side of the box the object sits in. It is a simple idea, but capable of enlivening a wall of storage and giving the user control over its final appearance.

Above The "Biblio-Theka (the man and his personal study)" is a shelf system created by the French designer Vincent Jalet while a student at London's Royal College of Art in 1998. The molded shelf units can be raised and lowered on a system of bands, and there are special parts to insert as modifications for CDs, magazines, and other things likely to be stored. It is adaptable, easily moved, and above all, fun.

HISTOIRE DES PALMIERS — Alain Durnerin

TASTE — Stephen Bayley

PHILIP COLLINS SMOKERAMA — CHRONICLE BOOKS

Éditions Champflour — ALAIN MOINIE — PALMIERS

Les Châteaux Viticoles du Pays de Vaud

Anne Willan — CHÂTEAU CUISINE — MACMILLAN

MONET'S TABLE — CLAIRE JOYES

Flammarion — James Darwen — La grande histoire du WHISKY

Flammarion — Bernard Le Roy / Maurice Szafran — CIGARE

FLAMMARION — YQUEM

The Vendome Press — CHÂTEAU MARGAUX

BANKING — GREEN

ABSINTHE — CON 830

Taste of ISRAEL

THE TASTE OF FRANCE

FRESON — La Colombe d'Or — Saint Paul de Vence — Éditions Assouline

MONTE-CARLO LA LEGENDE — EDITIONS ASSOULINE

THE ART OF THE CIGAR LABEL — DAVIDSON

CASTLEMAN — ART OF THE FORTIES

MICHEL SERRES — LA LEGENDE DES

Flammarion — FRA ANGELICO — DISSEMBLANCE ET FIGURATION

À SAINT-GERMAIN-DES-PRÉS

Kushner — MORGAN RUSSELL

Irving Penn — PASSAGE

DAVID

DAVID

PATRICE de MONCAN / CHRISTIAN MAHOUT — LES PASSAGE

JÉRUSALEM

O RIO ANTIGO

TIBET

Künkel — ELEPH

BOOKS FURNISH A ROOM

*B*ooks *Do Furnish a Room* is the title of a novel by
Anthony Powell from his sequence *A Dance to the
Music of Time.* It is supposed to have been inspired by the
laconic remark of a book reviewer when a pile of books fell
on him from shelves that could no longer bear the strain.
Most authors would like their books to do slightly more
than just furnish a room, yet books can have a value
beyond that of their content. When viewing titles on a
shelf, it is possible to form an immediate idea of the
owner's personality, and in this way books can be said to
help establish the look and feel of the room.

Not all homes contain books, and people at all levels
of society may live without them. The smart, if sterile,
drawing rooms of the 1930s, for example, seem to have
been adapted chiefly for drinking cocktails and reading
newspapers or magazines. By the same token, book-filled
rooms are not the prerogative of the socially privileged or
even of the highly educated. Anyone may possess books
and treasure them as part of their home.

Opposite A beautiful interior space in the
home of designers Charles and Ray Eames in
Santa Monica, California. The bookshelf has
been positioned to stand forward from the
wall (the ladder helps to emphasize this) and
has thus been turned into a spatial object,
rather like a miniature apartment block with
its own population of toys and model animals.

Below On a broad landing in the London
home of the architect Richard Rogers, books
are displayed on standard metal shelving, in
harmony with the stairs and stair rail. The
landing is large enough to allow chairs and
tables to be placed conveniently close to the
bookshelves, encouraging those who pass
by to stop for a while and browse.

A scattering of books, at least, is the mark of a civilized household. The barren rooms of the 1930s were superseded by a more "lived-in" look, a blend of old and new that followed the modernists in favoring a low level for seating, with tables to match, but allowed for a wide range of decorative expression. Broad circular tables between well-upholstered chairs gave room for a few piles of books and other essential accoutrements of relaxed reading, such as glasses or ashtrays, while table lamps cast a soft, diffused light. Books became part of a pleasing revival of clutter, which unlike much Victorian ephemera, was both beautiful and useful.

Such indulgence may have been largely replaced during the 1990s by a sharper modern look, but luckily the arid, bookless room has not come round again in the cycle of taste. Contemporary designers show considerable skill and ingenuity in accommodating books. Furthermore, books can be an important visual device for scaling down a large or high-ceilinged room, being by definition objects that can be held in the hand, belonging at a level of small detail that modern decoration can otherwise too easily eliminate. This is one of the most important ways in which they can be said to become part of the furnishing of an interior. As we return to the practices of our medieval ancestors and learn to live once again in large multi-purpose spaces, we are no longer constrained by the rules of decorum that existed in the more recent past, when books were segregated in special places of their own within the house, and often considered inappropriate in other rooms.

Far left The architect Ernö Goldfinger built this frame into the wall of his living room in Hampstead, London, in 1938. It serves for the display of pictures, sculptures, and large art books, all of which have a comfortable relationship to each other.

Left The New York apartment of the architect Paul Rudolph is a space full of excitement. In their nicely proportioned compartments beneath the overhanging gallery, the books look sufficiently disciplined not to disturb the rest of the room. It is always pleasant to have books immediately behind a seating area, where you can reach them without having to stand up.

Overleaf These dark-toned, leather-bound books are perfectly complemented by the heavy marble tabletop and its collection of ceramics and other objects. The framed photographs hung in front of the books add a personal, slightly surreal touch, and prevent the room from becoming too solemn.

75

The modern book is not necessarily a work of art, but generally has some kind of design quality. When visiting a house, or even looking at pictures of one in a magazine, it is hard not to read the titles on the spines of books to make a quick assessment of the character of the occupant. In addition, the design of the book jacket usually reflects something of the mood of the contents, which in turn establishes some of the character of the room. Some people are said to buy leather-bound books by the yard to impress others, but such tactics fool nobody. In any case, most of us no longer want to have all our books bound in the same style, because apart from the expense, it would be too boring, and individual books would be hard to find.

Right This set of shelves has a quality of tactile carpentry that is Japanese in feeling. The molded upstands at the ends of the shelves are both practical and elegant. The arrangement of books, turned wooden objects, and small pots accords with the sober character of the whole.

Opposite There have not been many innovations or modifications in the design of bookshelves, but Ron Arad's "Bookworm" is a completely novel solution, based more on fun than on functionalism. It has a sort of gravity-defying quality that makes you disbelieve at first, then work it out, then enjoy it.

Right It is not easy to take bookshelves around a corner, but this design succeeds in making the room feel complete. The warm, intimate atmosphere is not produced simply by the open fire and the many watching faces: the books themselves seem to enclose the room.

Left The strong but simple, floor-to-ceiling shelving in this house creates the feeling of a rustic cabin, which is reinforced by the stove. The minimalist effect of light and space depends largely on the absence of furniture and on the bare floors.

Below This room, characterized by rustic sophistication, would be an ideal place for the serious enjoyment of books. The main bookshelves look distinctly unsafe, but the precarious arrangement seems to match the room's casual bohemian style.

A COZY RETREAT

The idea of sitting down to read is one of the attractions of home. Books provide an inner warmth, while a fire in the room gives both real warmth and a kind of silent companionship. "Winter is the one time when I feel I can indulge myself in reading what I like instead of what I ought to read," wrote the poet John Betjeman, who for years made his living largely as a book reviewer. "While the storm shakes the shutters, I re-read Scott, generally starting with *The Heart of Midlothian*."

Reading time must now compete with many other pressures in life, including television and newer forms of electronic entertainment, but to read is to re-enter a world even older than the printed book, when tales were told around a fireside. That is one reason why it is an activity proper to the most often-used rooms in a home, and one for which provision of the right kind of natural or artificial light and other bodily comforts should always be considered essential and taken into account when planning a room.

Above Transparency gives a quality of mystery to this room, where the ultra-thin bookshelves have been left deliberately unfilled, and the colored pattern on the walls draws the eye through the spaces.

Left If solid shelves can be held up on such thin, almost invisible, wires, why don't we send all our possessions for a trip into space? The need to gain light from the window behind is the rationale for this act of levitation.

Far left These revolving shelves in the London apartment of writer Mario Vargas Llosa show how movable furniture can be used as a simple and instant means of reinventing an existing space. Rigged like ships in full sail, they make an original form of room divider.

BOOKS ON DISPLAY

"People say that life is the thing, but I prefer reading," said the essayist Logan Pearsall Smith. Books and works of art provide points of entry into other parallel worlds and can enjoy a peaceful coexistence. Even the Modernist architect Le Corbusier later modified his famous statement that a house is a machine for living in, by saying that it was also "*le lieu utile pour la meditation*" – a useful place for meditation.

If walls look bare without books, so also may tables. The "coffee-table book" is the only genre in publishing to acknowledge a direct relationship between books and interior furnishing. The term was originally used pejoratively to describe a book with more pictures than words, but this prejudice vanished long ago. Many books are now as much for browsing as for reading.

Opposite Books can be made an integral part of a living space by being housed in the depth of the wall, giving new meaning to the concept of built-in shelving. Hollow spaces in a wall, as seen here, are extremely useful, and all the better for not being shut off with doors or packed so full that the sense of depth is lost.

Below In this highly disciplined space, it seems fitting that the books are deeply recessed into the projecting paneled wall unit. Here, their bright colors can add a vibrant note without upsetting the overall harmony.

Books are made mostly of products derived from wood and have an affinity with this material, but when used for bookshelves, metal and glass – products favored by modernism in its heyday in the 1920s – can be very elegant, if not particularly cozy. Because of its strength, metal is often used to reduce the structure and create a more legible diagram of light and space, as in the classic tubular-steel furniture by designers such as Marcel Breuer, Charlotte Perriand, and Eileen Gray. Designs of this type, which are currently enjoying a revival, were intended to maximize space in small apartments and are therefore very appropriate for city loft living.

Right Some shelving systems can be purchased with boxlike units as well as shelves. Such a system has been used here to advantage, the solidity of the units contrasting with the lightweight metal structure of the uprights. The angled display shelves are ideal for book collectors who wish to display the front covers, not just the spines.

Left Isolated in space, this tall, geometric shelf unit achieves a sort of magisterial authority. The tall, slender pot in the foreground helps to emphasize the vertical orientation of the shelving and its independent, freestanding quality.

Above A modern interpretation of that literary cliché, the sliding bookcase. There might be more conventional ways of increasing book storage space, but this movable unit brings the whole wall to life and has a great sense of playfulness, despite its uniform white shelves.

88 *books furnish a room*

Left and below Sliding walls were a feature of early modern architecture, which broke the time-honored rules for the allocation of room functions and made possible a more flexible use of space. In this apartment, bookshelves act as sliding doors, dividing a living area from a home office.
The effect, seen both open and closed, is charming, original, and eminently practical.

The idea of bookshelves that move may seem paradoxical. These heavy objects are normally better left standing in one place. Yet the contradiction of a moving bookcase is somehow mysterious and exciting. How often in adventure stories does a section of the library bookcase swing silently back at the touch of a button to reveal the secret passage?

More prosaically, "jib" doors were used in former times to give servants access to the libraries of country houses, and were part of the fashion for making the decoration go round all four sides of the room without interruption. These doors were usually covered with fake book spines, often with joke titles. In modern interiors, where movable furniture is back in fashion, sliding or revolving bookcases have a somewhat different function. They increase the bookshelf space and at the same time make access to the books an amusing game. This type of shelving is also a way of adding interest to an interior, enabling the configuration of rooms to be altered as often as the occupants desire. A wall of books can sometimes become merely a flat space, but this can be prevented by creating two depths of shelves, with one set on runners.

BEYOND THE PALE

Readers do not normally select their books for color, but the traditional publishing practice in France and Italy has been to issue books in white paper wrappers, with the expectation that owners will have them individually bound. They are just as good, if not better, if left as they were in the shop. These "pre-paperbacks" are becoming less common as the years pass, although they can still be bought secondhand, while some French publishers bind their paperbacks in white covers in imitation of the old style. These books have always had the desirable quality of classics, unchanging through the years and unaffected by promotional graphic design, even of the most tasteful kind. If a few gaudy interlopers arrive, it is always possible to turn them around and leave only the white edges of the book on view. It is also possible, of course, to make plain paper covers for one's books, both for their protection and to achieve unity on the shelves. A line of old, limp vellum bindings in a historical library has the same quality of a white paint that is also warm to the touch.

White, a perennial color for interior design, has become increasingly popular in the current climate of minimalism, as it exposes textures to the passage of light and sharpens the senses to a greater degree of perception.

Above Not for ready reference: this beautiful still-life composition of limp, unbound French books with ivory objects is like a miniature city. The different tones of brown in the edges of the books, caused by acid deterioration, would distress a conservator but delight an aesthete.

Left Artfully artless: books piled anyhow in a fireplace make a feature in a room. The globe perhaps makes a reference to chaos and the cosmos, while the shelf brackets on the floor (shelves struggling to come into being) complete the surrealist ensemble.

Opposite "Curiouser and curiouser": real books and sculpted plaster dummies occupy the same set of shelves, merging the function of shelving into the art of decoration. Ghostly books at the back of the empty shelves create an illusion of space that extends even further back into a kind of looking-glass zone.

FOOD FOR THOUGHT

Books in dining rooms are good company. They make a sound-deadening background that is important in modern interiors, which often seem to be filled entirely with hard-surfaced furniture on a tiled floor, a style of interior design that looks stunning but may be unacceptably noisy. Books are also useful for settling points of fact or finding quotations in the middle of a meal, or for the entertainment of the solitary diner. It has been known for all members of a household to have a reading stand on the dinner table, although the idea of a family sitting down to meals together without the express wish to make conversation now seems odd.

A dining room usually contains the largest and most solid table in the house, which can easily double up as a library table. The two functions are thoroughly compatible, although the disadvantage of this arrangement is that you may have to clear your current research project off the table before a dinner party and find somewhere else to put it.

As Sydney Smith, the wittiest Englishman of the Regency period, once said, there is "no furniture so charming as books."

Below Formal symmetry without explicit classicism makes this a room that combines stimulation and relaxation. Crucial to its success are the tall, isolated bookshelves, which flank the double doors rather than merging with the display shelves.

Above These are unit shelves of the simplest kind, yet they still create a feeling of calm and order with their long, extended horizontal lines. The lighting beneath the main shelves is an old trick that helps to bring the room to life after dark.

Left A scholarly library, housed in simple timber bookshelves, creates a sense of security appropriate to the enjoyment of good food and wine. The shelves are well matched to the table, with its fine grain figure on the surface and its interesting construction beneath.

books furnish a room **93**

ARTIST'S BOOKS

While the vast majority of books today are printed and bound by machine, the crafts of fine printing and bookbinding are flourishing with a new artistic freedom. The people who make these objects are no longer competing against mass production but occupying themselves with the production of unique objects or small batches, in which the quality of craftsmanship and materials is matched by new ideas.

The term "artist's book" was traditionally used to mean simply a fine illustrated edition, often with signed original prints, but today's version is more often than not a fully three-dimensional work, involving a range of possible binding, printing, and papermaking techniques. It is an exciting field for collectors, as the works are often modestly priced compared to paintings or sculptures, but relatively easy to transport, store, and display.

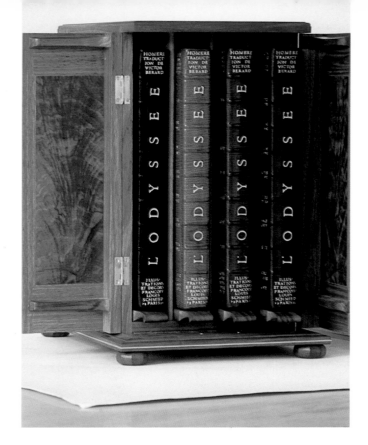

Above *The Odyssey*, bound by Roger Powell in 1955 and housed in a special box. Powell was one of the pioneers of fine craft binding in Britain, and was responsible for valuable rescue work after the Florence floods in 1966.

Left A pop-up book for grown-ups, *Bluebeard's Castle* (1972), by Ron King. This work features a simple presentation for a complex idea, using techniques normally reserved for children's books.

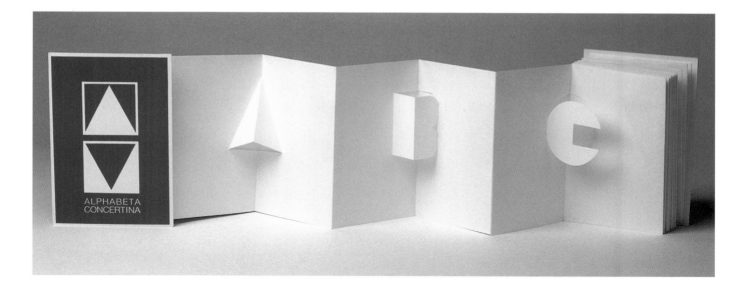

Left Poems by the Greek poet C.P. Cavafy, bound in 1988 by Romilly Saumarez-Smith. The use of colored inlays in leather is a favorite technique among modern binders. The subtle, abstract imagery of the binding gives it a status, independent of the text inside, as a piece of design and craftsmanship.

Above Ron King's *Alphabeta Concertina* (1983) is a sophisticated three-dimensional toy, using the techniques of cutting and folding paper pioneered at the Bauhaus. It makes the metaphorical building blocks of language look literally like building blocks.

Right An artist's book, *2 Walks* by Les Bicknell (1993), produced in a limited edition of seven. In this project the text, images, printing techniques, and binding form part of an indistinguishable whole, so that the imagery and lettering seem to have grown out of the rough handmade paper, rather than to have been printed on.

KITCHENS

Of all the rooms in the house, the kitchen has seen its function change the most in the last thirty years. It is still the place where food is prepared and cooked, but until the end of the 1960s, this was probably all that was done there. Now, when at home, many people spend the greater part of their time in the kitchen. To meet this need, the kitchen has absorbed elements of the dining room, playroom, and family sitting room. As a result, we are likely to lavish more money on it than on any other room in the house.

These changes came about largely through the re-creation of what was vaguely thought to be the "farmhouse kitchen," a much larger room than the small galley with hygienic hi-tech fittings previously seen as the epitome of modern living. Although the nostalgic farmhouse style has been reinterpreted in various ways, today's kitchen designers continue to respond to the need for diversity of function. Cookbooks have undergone a similar transformation in recent years. Nowadays they are more often than not large format and packed with colorful photographs, and reflect a wide range of lifestyles and interests. They are an essential part of any contemporary kitchen, and housing them to proper effect demands both ingenuity and visual flair.

Left The central "island" in this kitchen has been beautifully made and is an ideal place for storing a small collection of cookbooks and magazines. There is little risk of the books coming into contact with food as it is prepared, since they are kept well out of the way and protected from spills by the overhanging work surface.

Far left In a modern kitchen, books need to be kept in their place but should also combine with other objects in the room to suggest both culinary skill and individual style. This kitchen has been carefully planned to give plenty of storage for books and cooking utensils, which are close at hand on shelves and in cabinets under the work area.

Above Cookbooks should be reachable when needed, and keeping them in a cabinet under the work surface is an eminently practical solution where there is insufficient space for a bookshelf. The curved white doors of this streamlined unit contrast with the lines of the floorboards and add a distinctive touch of style to the kitchen.

Even before the Second World War brought an effective end to traditional domestic service for all but the very rich, the cook had begun to disappear from the middle-class household. Cooking now needed to be given a more attractive image, one that was reflected in the cookbooks of the period. Heavyweight volumes like Mrs. Beeton's *Book of Household Management* were increasingly seen as obsolete. In their place came books that were decorative as well as practical. Among the most attractive was the series written by Ambrose Heath, with illustrations by Edward Bawden, although the recipes now seem needlessly elaborate. After the war, food writing was revolutionized by the English author Elizabeth David, whose early books had illustrations by John Minton. David gave the world a firsthand insight into French bourgeois home cooking, in sharp contrast to the *haute cuisine* served in restaurants.

In modern times, cookbooks have topped the lists of bestsellers. Lavishly illustrated with mouthwatering photography, they are often written by "personalities" who are also cooks and by cooks who have become "personalities." Cooking is now a popular leisure activity, and few kitchens are completely bookless. Even those who rely on prepared meals from the supermarket, or on pizza or Chinese food delivered to their door, must at least sustain the illusion that they could, if necessary, rustle up something simple but sophisticated.

Above It is not necessary for every book in a kitchen to be a cookbook – this kitchen is a home for library overspill. The well-proportioned wall fitting also houses a wine rack, tableware, and other utensils, and has a pleasing quality of "a place for everything and everything in its place."

Left A design feature in its own right, the metal rail puts the tools of the cook's trade within easy reach. The lecternlike rack hanging from the rail is an ingenious device for holding storage jars, and can be hooked on wherever it is needed.

Left Fine china, books, and food are three of the good things in life, and this storage system combines them all in generous quantities, without losing sight of design discipline. The checker-patterned tiles reinforce the lines of the shelving.

THE PRACTICAL KITCHEN

Cookbooks that are in regular use should be kept close at hand in the kitchen. However many there are, it will probably be most practical to house them all in the same place, together with such items as boxed recipe cards and notebooks or files containing recipes cut out of newspapers and magazines. Shelving for books should be either above or below the work surface, although like almost everything else in the kitchen, it is a matter of what feels comfortable and easy to work with. Those who like to think of everything may have a reading stand to rest the book on while following recipe instructions, perhaps with grips to hold the pages open.

Above For all its emphasis on metal surfaces and reflection, this kitchen is the hub of the home, a place for pleasure as well as work.

Left Cupboard doors open to reveal an artfully disordered array of crockery and books.

Right Books have been welcomed into the heart of this kitchen and invited to sit down. This is an informal arrangement that offers effective access to the books, but it might prove less than practical if the table is in constant use for food preparation.

Left A neat vertical arrangement of books in the corner of a kitchen. The ones on the top shelf look as if they may not be used very often, but how many people use more than half a dozen cookbooks in the normal course of life? The reading stand on the counter top is a clever additional gadget, allowing for both the display and protection of favorite books.

Below Books under the counter: a little leftover space is enough for an adequate kitchen library. But remember that you will need a sufficient shelf depth to ensure that larger books do not project too far and prevent drawers and cabinets from opening.

Books in the kitchen need to be kept apart from the messier aspects of the cooking process, but luckily there are not normally so many of them as to make this a problem. They add a welcome touch of variety and even their titles and spines can stimulate the appetite and promise pleasures of the table. A certain used quality is quite permissible: many cookbooks have strong personal associations, recalling different eras of life, from first apartment to house and family.

Most kitchens today are custom-designed down to the last inch, so that there is no excuse for leaving out book spaces. A shelf for books and a shelf for pots or china are much the same. The only constraint seems to be that while kitchen equipment may be hidden in cupboards, books are normally expected to be found out in the open. They certainly help to prevent a feeling of perfect hygiene and efficiency from crushing life and individuality out of the room. We could be sure that the mother of the unfortunate boy in Jacques Tati's film *Mon Oncle*, who puts on rubber gloves to cook her child's prepackaged food, would not tolerate anything as dirty as a book to pollute her clinical cooking space, but you can always keep the books behind glass doors.

Left A varied set of shelves gives several book storage options. This collection looks informal and well used, a promise of good food to come that should be as convincing as any advanced *batterie-de-cuisine*.

Overleaf The wrought-iron stand in this Mediterranean-style kitchen provides an unusual but effective solution for storing books alongside bottles, plants, and even hats.

FURNITURE

BOOKS AS

Designers have the opportunity to play with books as objects in a number of ways. In the process, the intrinsic quality of the book may well be subverted and challenged, but the result can be a renewed appreciation of books, or perhaps a realization that they become tyrants if allowed to rule our lives. It is too easy to accept them as simply benign or neutral objects. Controversial issues such as censorship make them anything but neutral.

In the pieces shown here, the British designer and artist Ralph Ball works on our reactions and feelings by introducing a deliberate quality of alienation. On a basic level, this alienation is mostly due to the fact that the viewer is unable to actually open or read any of the books involved, which alters our expectation and hints at ideas of waste and misuse. Ball challenges our beliefs about the sacredness of books and subverts their meaning as carriers of information by turning them into furniture components and rendering them useless as anything else.

Below *Coffee Table Book Table (Self Adjusting)*, from 1997, comments on the incestuous relationship between design and books on design, which are often produced in greater numbers than the actual objects that they illustrate. The books are all copies of the International Design Yearbook, built up year by year. Ball writes: "each successive edition renders the previous one redundant, confined in an inaccessible archive."

Left *Information Storage* (1998) comments on the way that high-tech methods of storing information might seem to be superseding such traditional sources of information as the book. This is symbolized by the way the four books are stacked in a way that books never normally are, and are pierced with slits to form a CD rack. As a result, the books in this piece have gone from being an information storage system in their own right to acting as a storage unit for other information storage systems.

Right In *The Complete History of Shelf Supports* (1998), four volumes of a fictional multi-volume work perform the function that the titles describe. The result is not so much a piece of furniture as a visual joke, in which the shelf is supported by the books instead of the other way around. The concept is taken further by the fact that the titles of the books indicate that the shelf is being supported not by mere books, but by every type of shelf support that ever existed.

BEDROOMS AND BATHROOMS

Those people whose book collection has already spread into every other part of the house will see bedrooms and bathrooms as a perfect opportunity to extend their library. The bedroom is, in any case, many people's preferred reading room. Writing about the English middle-class home circa 1900, the German architect Herman Muthesius assumed there would be "a small table for books" in every bedroom. More than this he would probably have thought to be contrary to the "healthy freshness…evocative of freshly laundered linen" that he considered essential in a well-planned bedroom. But the keynote of the bedroom ought to be comfort rather than hygienic necessity. Books in bedrooms are indeed comforting, especially for those who cannot get into bed without at least three books beside them in case of sudden nocturnal literary deprivation. The knowledge that without leaving the room you can have access to several hundred more is a perfect way to remove stress and anxiety and induce relaxation.

Below Clarity and comfort in an all-white bedroom. Shelves, containing an assortment of books and other objects, line the wall behind the head of the monumental bed. The juxtaposition of bed and shelves creates a book-lined passageway.

Left Next to the bed, but not too close for comfort, a deep shelf makes a compact but convenient study space in this curvaceous room in a 1930s modernist house. The custom-built storage unit curves with the wall, and its line is repeated in the skylight and headboard.

Above A bedroom that has two windows can spare one of them, which in this case is concealed behind a screen of books stretching from floor to ceiling. This clever idea maximizes the storage space in a well-planned bedroom, while still letting in light from behind the shelves.

Above The interior of architect Richard Rogers' London home, which dates from the nineteenth century, has been created by stripping out walls, fixtures, and fittings. His and her books are conveniently at hand on shelves cut deep into the bed surround.

Right This house in Hampstead, London was designed in 1938 by Ernö Goldfinger and is now open to the public. The shelves in the bedroom are standard units braced between floor and ceiling. They dominate the room but also emphasize its calm aura.

There can be no fixed principles for designing shelves in bedrooms, except perhaps to avoid reproducing too closely the character of a library. A little more imagination is permissible. Books running behind or over the head of the bed, or over a doorway, are conveniently close at hand, yet also create a pleasingly unexpected feature in a room. A single shelf that runs right around the room beneath a low ceiling provides a unified design, but will work only when none of the books is much bigger than a standard paperback. A wall entirely covered with books is likely to dominate a bedroom but can also act as a protective cocoon in which the occupant feels safe and can relax easily.

Above Strong paint color used for the shelves enlivens the faded bindings of the books in an English country bedroom. The shelf carried over the door is an important feature in the room, completing the architectural effect.

Right Imaginatively constructed shelves fit neatly between work surfaces in a child's bedroom. The shelves accommodate toys as well as books, and make creative use of the space by projecting at a right angle from the wall.

Below The fireplace in this bedroom has been cleverly adapted to act as a bookcase, with shelves of varying heights. Ascending by balloon in the picture over the mantelpiece are Babar and Celeste, the elephants in Jean de Brunhof's famous series of children's books.

CHILDREN'S ROOMS

Children's bedrooms will probably house much of their personal book collection. Books and toys can get muddled up together and there is plenty of scope for fun and fantasy when planning cupboards and bookshelves. Some children's classics, like the stories of Beatrix Potter, have a distinctive small format, and the child may own enough titles in a series to warrant building a shelf especially to fit them. Other picture books, including such classic series as Jean de Brunhoff's *Babar* or Ludwig Bemelmans' *Madeline*, come in much larger sizes and will be too tall for many shelves. Most children do not have enough books of this sort to fill a whole shelf, anyway, so it may be best to lay them horizontally. Computers and televisions are now as common as books in children's rooms, and a storage system may need to accommodate these also.

Many children's classics are now "merchandized," allowing a child to enjoy them in a number of different ways. Items such as clothes, stuffed toys, and toothbrushes may all be themed around favorite books, and the practice may also extend to the decoration of the bedroom itself, with book and cartoon characters appearing on duvet covers and other soft furnishings, lightshades, wallpaper, and even rugs.

Overleaf The bookcases in this bathroom, coupled with the stuffed birds, turn it into an unorthodox extension of the Victorian gentleman's library.

Below This busy room has plenty of concealed storage, in which books take their place amid a great variety of objects. Like Max's bedroom in Maurice Sendak's *Where the Wild Things Are*, the room feels as if it might turn into a forest at night.

BATHROOMS

Adopting a horizontal posture while reading can be very conducive to creative thought, and a bathtub can serve as well as a bed – or better, if one believes those psychologists who claim that water has both mental and physical curative properties. Is there a particular type of book that is suited to bathroom reading? A small format is obviously an advantage, and there is currently a trend toward miniaturization in book design. Collections of cartoons are commonly found in bathrooms, but this room is also an ideal place for poetry, to be read in short bursts. The humid atmosphere seems to do little damage to books, although it is obviously important not to fall asleep and drop the book in the water. A book rest set up next to the bathtub is an obvious solution to the problem and an ideal bathroom accessory for the dedicated reader.

A bathroom can also be used to display poster poems like those seen on trains in the New York subway and other transport systems around the world. They provide a personalized thought for the day or a memory exercise to learn in the bath, and are quick and cheap to make. Simply enlarge the poem on a photocopier or type it to the correct size on a computer, and insert in a plastic clip frame.

Left The bathroom as an extension of the home office. Bathing and business don't usually mix, but this is a neat way of storing pamphlets, catalogs, and magazines, which might be consulted while in the bath, to make bathtime more productive.

Above One of the advantages of bathtubs over showers is that they allow for reading. A book rest is not yet a standard fixture in a bathroom, but this sturdy chrome stand removes all risk of accidental submersion and will appeal to bathtime book lovers.

Right Books should always be available close at hand when and where they are needed. This lavatory-cum-library is a perfect illustration of this principle, housing a nostalgic array of old paperbacks, with shelves custom-built to fit them.

BOOK PLATES

There is a long tradition of using individual bookplates as a mark of ownership, originating from the time when books were valuable treasures to be cherished and closely guarded. These markers usually combine words and images, sometimes for an individual, sometimes for an institution. The images used may be a play on the person's name, a representation of their profession, or a more subtle interpretation of their interests. Bookplates commonly use the Latin term "*Ex Libris*" ("from the library"). In continental Europe, collectors traditionally commissioned a succession of bookplates from different artists, with a special category of erotic bookplates. Artists can draw and print images in a number of ways, but the small scale of the bookplate lends itself especially well to the technique of wood engraving.

Above Two wood engravings for simple bookplates by Enid Marx, who had a long career as a designer in England from the 1920s to the 1990s working on projects ranging from book jackets and postage stamps to upholstery for London Transport. The bookplate on the right was designed for the owner of Selbourn Books (hence the "S"), who had a particular interest in fruit growing.

Far Left A colored woodcut with an elaborate Renaissance-inspired interior dominates this early twentieth-century German book plate by Ernst Liebermann. The lettering is subtly designed to look as if it is carved out of stone.

Left A bookplate by Aubrey Beardsley, the most famous English illustrator of the 1890s. Beardsley's typical aura of decadence is elegantly achieved with flat black-and-white graphics, a style particularly appropriate to reproduction by photo-etched line block. In this case, the image definitely takes precedence over the lettering.

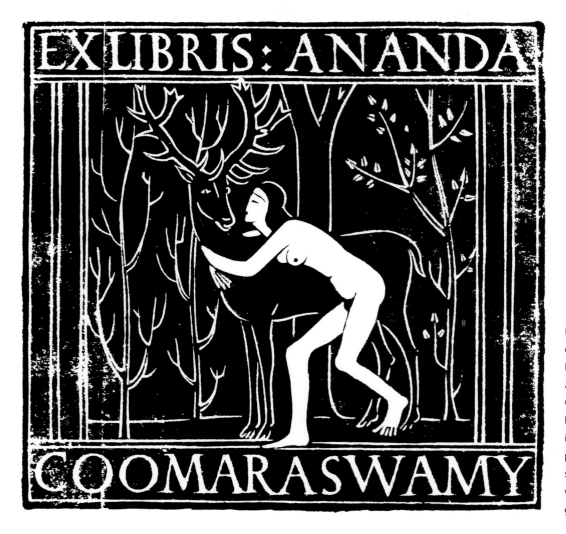

Left The British artist Eric Gill designed and engraved this bookplate for the philosopher and art historian Ananda Coomaraswamy in 1920. It has a simple directness in its imagery, lettering, and style, producing an effect that is slightly naive but executed with the confidence of a graphic master.

Right Two bookplates by Berthold Wolpe, a designer who came from Germany to Britain as a refugee from Hitler in 1938. He always used an economic but striking black-and-white graphic style to convey his visual message.

CARE AND MAINTENANCE

Books are remarkably tough and resilient in most conditions, provided they are handled with reasonable care. The rules for conserving most kinds of objects apply equally to books – not too much light and not too much heat. Take extra care if you live in a hot, humid place, as mildew can grow on books very quickly in such an environment. On the other hand, books are happy in relatively cold and humid conditions, although this should not be carried too far. It is when they are moved abruptly from one environmental condition to another that problems are most likely to appear.

The quality of book production has been through various historical cycles. The period between 1850 and 1900 was responsible for poor, acidic paper and weak bindings, often intended to make a cheap but showy product, but books from other periods ought to withstand both time and usage.

Regular maintenance should normally involve little more than removing dust from the top edges of books, where it invariably settles. This is best done with a vacuum cleaner, with a piece of cheesecloth across the end as a filter to keep anything valuable from going down the tube. Leather bindings may be oiled occasionally if kept in dry conditions, but more damage will be done by over-oiling than by neglect.

Repairs to pages and bindings need to be given careful thought, with professional advice from a conservator if the book is of any value. "Leave well alone" is the best motto, and make only small interventions to prevent

Right Books at Felbrigg Hall in Norfolk, England, a house once owned by a notable scholar and author. Books are seen here displayed alongside other items of beauty and historic interest.

Left A valuable collection of illustrated antiquarian books, with fold-out engraved illustrations. The quality of rag paper in early books was remarkable, and they normally require less conservation than the products of later periods, when inferior materials and mass production techniques were used.

deterioration – preferably ones that can be reversed or removed harmlessly in the future. This rules out most kinds of adhesive tape. For weakened or damaged bindings of important books, it is better to have a box specially made that also helps to keep them in a clean, acid-free environment. Paper covers and wrappers can be made more simply, and these are both protective and decorative. You can encase dust jackets, which usually add to the value and interest of books, in transparent plastic sleeves.

Water is one of the worst enemies of books. A single wetted book should be interleaved with absorbent paper immediately and allowed to dry slowly. A whole flooded library should be freeze-dried prior to rescue. Pests are also a problem, not only the proverbial bookworm but cockroaches and even rodents.

Keep acidic materials away from books, and particularly avoid sticking acidic paper inside their pages. Although it is fun to put newspaper cuttings, letters, and ephemera in books ("loosely inserted" is the bookseller's catalog phrase), this can be overdone and cause damage to the binding.

A new hazard for books is the self-stick note. These do not necessarily make any visible marks, but they can discolor paper and also leave a sticky patch that picks up dirt and dust. They do not work any better than slips of paper for making notes, so stick to the old way of doing things.

When handling books, use common sense. Have clean hands; keep food and drink at a distance. Open heavy books on a table or stand. Do not wedge books too tightly into shelves and avoid pulling them by the normally rather fragile head of the spine. Turn the pages lightly from the corner and use a thin paper bookmark to keep a place. Be careful of the binding when photocopying and do not force a book open.

These are only hints and broad principles. There are good sources of information about book conservation and a growing number of professionals. If you love books in any way, looking after them becomes a natural extension of that love.

THE BASICS

PROJECTS

This section offers a range of do-it-yourself options for creating book storage. These vary from store-bought self-assembly systems to making a pine bookcase from scratch. None of the projects are beyond the capability of a novice, providing adequate time and care are taken. Please note that all measurements are in millimeters to allow for the greatest precision. For those new to woodworking, an introductory book on carpentry will be of great value. Some of the projects need little more than an electric drill, while others are more complex. The key to effective woodworking is not having a lot of equipment but rather having a few tools in good condition. Having a saw sharpened, buying and honing a new plane iron ("blade"), or replacing

blunt drill bits will save hours of frustration later. Tool lists are given for each project but it is worth making some notes about tools in general. Many saws are now designed to be effectively disposable. They are fairly inexpensive and do not need sharpening. A smoothing plane is essential and these do need regular sharpening on either an oil stone or water stone, available from hardware stores. For many projects, a miter saw (used for cutting the ends of more than one piece at equal angles) will be very useful, while a honing guide (a wedge-shaped clamp device), also available from hardware stores, will enable you to get the correct angle for the best results. You will also need some kind of work bench with a vise.

Two types of shelving that are readily available in do-it-yourself and home furnishing stores, and that only need screwing together before use, are illustrated on these two pages. The "flatpack" pine bookcase shown opposite is freestanding, and therefore it is the most straightforward project for the complete beginner as it requires no special tools other than a screwdriver, and needs no wall attachments. The rack system shown below, on the other hand, is wall-mounted, and requires a little more planning. The safety of wall-mounted bookshelves, which can be very heavy when fully loaded, is dependent on the security of the wall fixings. Following the correct sequence of simple steps, as illustrated and discussed on the right, will help you achieve long-lasting and accurate results.

◀ Hold the piece to be mounted up to the wall using a spirit level to check that it is correctly positioned. Rather than marking the hole positions with a pencil, tap a screw through each of the screw points in the wood with a hammer so that it makes an indentation in the wall. This provides a location for the drill bit and prevents it from wandering across the surface of the plaster. Brick walls sound solid when tapped, while plasterboard sounds hollow.

◀ The wall plug shown is designed for a brick wall. For plasterboard, you will need special plugs that are designed to open out like an umbrella when inserted into the space behind the plasterboard, to keep from slipping out again. Plasterboard is quite thin and not particularly strong, so if a bookshelf is to be mounted on it, use plenty of well-spaced screws. When drilling, set the depth stop on the drill to allow for a hole the length of the plug plus 3mm, and use a sharp masonry bit.

◀ Insert the plugs into the holes. If they do not push all the way in, clean out any dust from the hole or bore it slightly deeper. Wall plugs and screws must be compatible, for example a 6mm diameter plug and No. 8 screw is a good working combination. As a rule of thumb, the depth of the screw in the wall should be about twice the thickness of the rail being fitted. Put screws in all hole positions in the piece being mounted and locate them in their wall plugs. This will ensure that all the screws are properly fitted. Finally, drive the screws in tight.

METAL RACK

This bookcase offers a different approach to making your own book storage. There is no wood work and little in the way of practical skill is required at all, apart from drilling holes and sawing some metal strips to length. You may need to look a little further afield for the materials than your local do-it-yourself store. The extruded aluminum pieces for the frame can be sourced through aluminum dealers in your area. Threaded rod and the appropriate nuts are available from most hardware stores. Galvanized wire is used to tension the structure. This will require loops at each end and a rigging screw in each length, and four shackles to fit the wires. All of this can be made up to order by a yacht-supply retailer. None of the metal work needs any finish, and it will create a high-tech nautical effect.

Various materials could be used for the shelves. Rough, bare wood could provide a contrast to the metal while retaining the nautical theme; painted plywood or glass are two further options. If you choose glass it should be at least 20mm thick, and the edges should be polished by the supplier. Thick glass has a blue-green cast that is particularly appropriate for this project. Be warned though that glass is more expensive than wood.

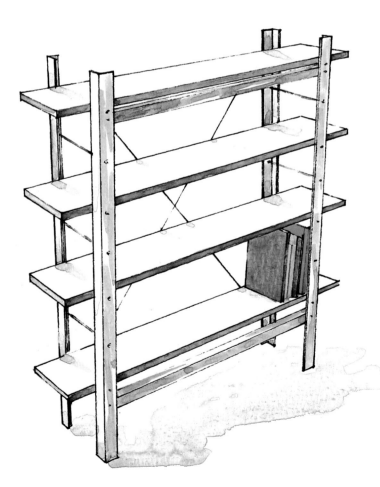

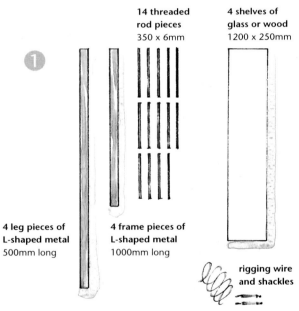

14 threaded rod pieces
350 x 6mm

4 shelves of glass or wood
1200 x 250mm

4 leg pieces of L-shaped metal
500mm long

4 frame pieces of L-shaped metal
1000mm long

rigging wire and shackles

▲ Cut the metal extrusions and threaded rods to length using a hacksaw or, alternatively, a miter saw. You will also need a vise for this job. File the ends of the metal pieces smooth. File each end of the threaded rod and try fitting a nut on each end to ensure that no burrs (rough areas) remain in the thread. Solid wood shelves should be 25–30mm thick and plywood 25mm thick to prevent them bowing under a load.

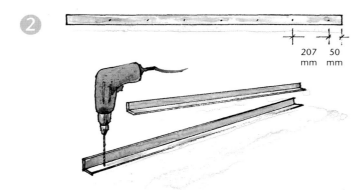

◄ Use a plywood strip cut to the same length as the uprights as a template for drilling the holes. Mark out the hole positions on the template and drill holes the same diameter as the threaded rod. Tape this to each upright in turn and drill the holes through. Drill both sides of each hole with a countersink (a drill bit that enlarges the top of a drill hole to allow screw heads to sink flush) to remove any burrs.

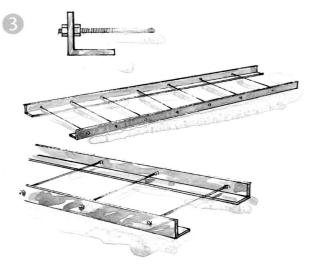

► Begin assembly by fitting a nut to each end of the threaded rods, making sure they are all equally spaced (see detail). Insert into one leg and fit the opposing nuts. Repeat the process to complete the end frames. Once assembled check that the uprights are parallel and tighten up the structure with a wrench.

◄ Mark the positions of the crossbars. Drill the holes in the uprights first and again countersink to remove the burrs. The crossbars fit inside the angle section of the uprights. Hold them in place (with a small "G" clamp if you have one) and drill through from the outside. Join the bars together with a short length of threaded rod about 25mm long placed through the drilled holes with a nut at each end.

▼ Do not order the rigging wire until you know exactly how long the pieces need to be. Bore a hole in each end of the cross bars to take the shackle. Fit the loops at the ends of the wires to the cross bars with the shackles. To prevent the frame from becoming distorted, the rigging screws need to be tightened up evenly. The detail shown below right illustrates the arrangement of components inside the top corner.

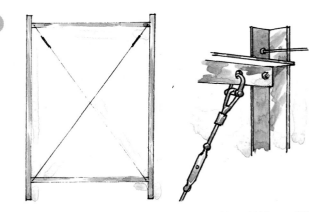

STAIRCASE SHELF

The idea for this project came from the observation that some people use their staircase as an ad hoc library. Indeed it would fit neatly over or under a staircase or in many other difficult-to-use spaces. Several could be mounted on the same wall to form an interesting focal point. This is the simplest of the woodworking projects featured here and would be a good introduction for a novice woodworker before trying something more advanced. Plywood or solid wood may be used. If you choose solid wood, the screw holes will need to be counterbored with a bigger hole and a wooden plug fitted to hide the screw head using a matching drill/plug cutter set.

Many large do-it-yourself stores provide a wood-cutting service. Even if you are confident of your ability to cut wood straight and square, having the job done at the source is likely to be a lot quicker. An accurately prepared cutting list is fundamental to the success of any woodworking project. Solid wood requires more work than plywood, so there is little point in using it if you intend to paint the finished piece. However, there are a number of finishes that enhance the natural characteristics of solid timber. A simple wax finish leaving the wood in its natural color is difficult to improve on, but a wash of dilute emulsion paint will introduce color without obscuring the grain of the timber. This can then be polished with a clear finishing wax. Alternatively, you can use stain to darken the wood and accentuate its natural features. Suggestions for painted finishes suitable for plywood are given on p. 134.

1

300mm

▲ All the pieces are square and the same size. The size marked on the illustration above is only a suggestion. The wood should be 20–25mm, thick enough to take the screws but not so thick that it becomes too heavy. It is important to prepare the timber accurately so that the ends of the pieces fit together smoothly to make up the butt joints that form the construction of the whole shelf unit.

◄ Carefully mark out the screw hole positions with an awl (a tool for piercing wood) to provide a positive location for the drill bit. A hole 4.5mm in diameter will be needed to take the shank of a No. 8 wood screw. Then countersink the hole to take the head of the screw. If you do not wish the head of the screw to be visible, it should be countersunk deep enough to allow filler to be applied over the top. If you are using solid wood, you will need to counterbore the hole to take a wooden plug.

► To assemble, hold the upright part of the "staircase" vertically in the vise and align the horizontal part so that the screw positions can be marked. Bore pilot holes either with an awl or preferably with a 3mm drill bit. Screwed end-grain joints are not particularly strong, so the screws should be at least 50mm long. Apply glue to both sides of the joint. Any wood glue will suffice, but PVA glue is the simplest to use. Drive in the screws and wipe off excess glue with a damp cloth.

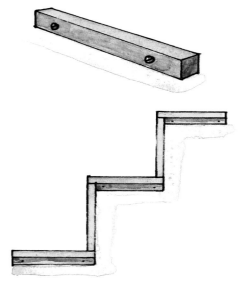

◄ Use strips of wood to fix the shelf to the wall. These should be 19mm square in thickness. Mark the lengths of the strips against the underside of the shelf. Bore two holes to fit the strips to the shelf and two more at 90-degree angles to fit the bookshelf to the wall. Once assembled, plane the outside faces of the joints flush. Fill the screw holes with an epoxy filler (ordinary wood filler will not adhere to the screw heads). Sand the whole unit smooth before applying the finish of your choice.

STACKING BOX

This simple idea is very versatile, and the sizes of the boxes can be chosen to suit your specific needs. Used as a single unit, it would make a desktop bookcase, while several stacked together could form a room divider. The construction develops the "Staircase" project (pp.132–133) by attaching two butt joints to form a box. Plywood about 18–25mm thick would be a good material for this project. The sides of the boxes may be any size within reason. You could paint the boxes a single color to fit in with the existing décor of a room. Alternatively, for a more adventurous effect, you could choose a number of complementary colors, or two vividly contrasting colors. The number of kits and instruction books available on the subject means that many painting techniques and effects are now easy for the home decorator to achieve. As with any finish, a well-prepared surface is the key to a good result. For small jobs, hand sanding is an efficient way of preparing a surface. With bigger pieces of furniture, the hard work of preparing the bare wood and sanding lightly between coats of finish can be done by machine. A random orbital sander is ideal for this and well worth the investment if you intend to do a lot of work, or you may be able to rent one by the day from a do-it-yourself store.

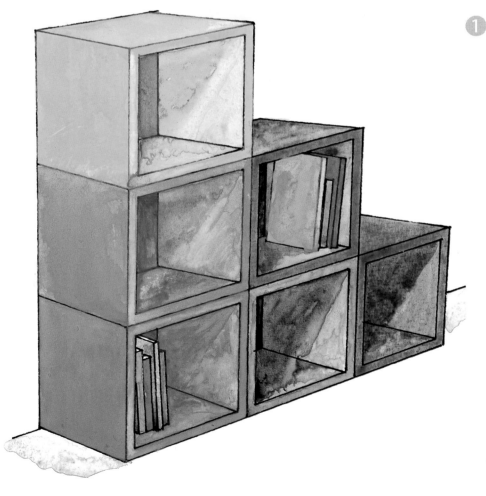

plywood box sides
350 x 350mm

plywood box backs
350 x 350 x 6mm

▲ For the sides of the box, start with prepared and sanded plywood cut to your chosen dimensions. The backs are also of plywood but much thinner than the main side pieces. Note that the holes should be marked and drilled in one end of each of the sides of the box. Once the hole positions have been marked on one piece, this can be used as a template for the others. If you are making several boxes, make a 6mm plywood template with the holes bored in the correct places. You can place this onto each piece in turn and drill the holes through the template.

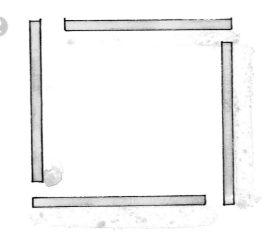

②

◀ To assemble the pieces, you will need a vise. Countersink the holes to take the screw heads and align the joint so that pilot holes for the screws can be bored. The detail below left shows a cross section of the screwed joint. Use a PVA wood glue on both faces of the joint. When all four sides have been assembled, wipe off any excess glue with a damp cloth.

③

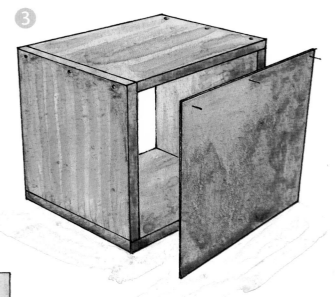

▶ Plane the edges of the joints flush with the sides of the box. The front and back edges also need to be planed to ensure a neat front and a flat back face to take the back panel. The back should be cut 2–3mm oversize all around and pinned and glued in place. Use 20mm panel nails. When the glue is entirely dry, plane the edges of the back flush with the cabinet.

④

◀ Fill the screw holes with epoxy filler. This is a two-part filler with a separate hardener. It is sold as a wood filler but is the same as car body filler. It adheres well and sands nicely. Sand all outside faces and round over the edges slightly in preparation for painting. The edges of plywood can be a problem when a clean painted surface is desired, as the laminates tend to show through the paint. You can avoid this by coating the edges with filler and sanding them smooth.

CANTILEVER RACK

Balance rather than wall-mounting is the principle of this project – the rack simply leans against the wall. A set of shelves like this will need to be placed on a carpet as the friction will keep the unit from sliding across the floor, or if you do not have carpet you could fit the bottoms of the uprights with rubber feet.

The shelves slide into slots and are not mechanically fitted. Though the concept is simple, this project needs careful preparation. The slots must be very accurately made in order to work properly, as the shelves need to slide in easily but fit snugly. The upright frames are of solid wood, which must be perfectly straight. Plywood or solid wood may be used for the shelves. The piece may be stained and polished, but a painted finish is not appropriate, as the thickness of the paint will affect the way the shelves fit into the slots. It would be best to use the measurements shown here, but if this does not provide enough space, two or three identical bookcases could be used side by side to create a bigger storage system.

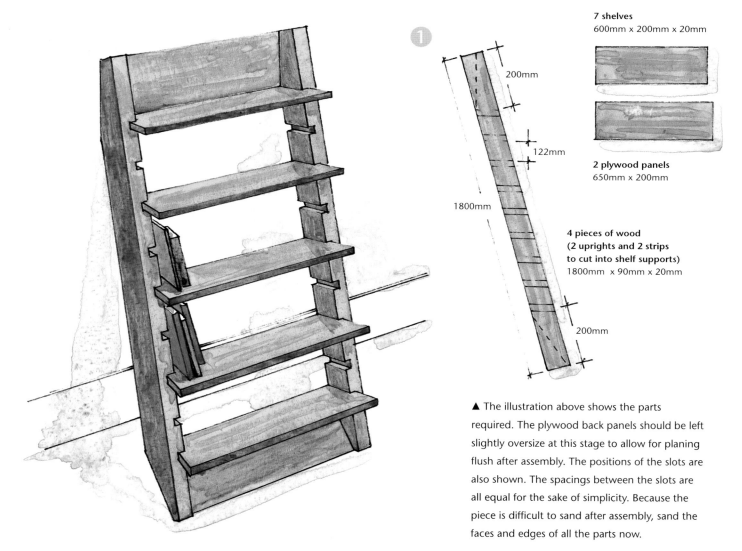

7 shelves
600mm x 200mm x 20mm

200mm

122mm

1800mm

2 plywood panels
650mm x 200mm

4 pieces of wood
(2 uprights and 2 strips
to cut into shelf supports)
1800mm x 90mm x 20mm

200mm

▲ The illustration above shows the parts required. The plywood back panels should be left slightly oversize at this stage to allow for planing flush after assembly. The positions of the slots are also shown. The spacings between the slots are all equal for the sake of simplicity. Because the piece is difficult to sand after assembly, sand the faces and edges of all the parts now.

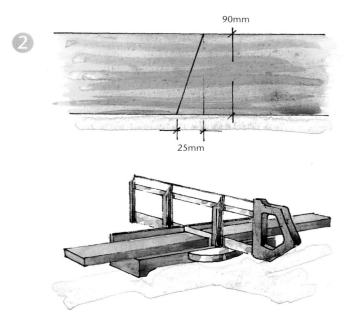

90mm

25mm

◄ Cut two of the long rails into angled blocks. A miter saw (shown bottom left), while not essential, will make this task much easier. The saw can be set at the right angle and its guide bars will ensure a perfectly true cut. One advantage of these saws is that the teeth are much finer than on an average saw and they produce a very fine finish. The cut surface will need no more than a light sanding.

▶ Pin the blocks with panel nails and glue them into place. Before you do this, drill pilot holes the same diameter as the panel nails into the small blocks to prevent them from splitting when you put the nails in. Mark the positions of the blocks on the upright rails as a guide. An offcut of the material to be used for the shelves will serve as a spacing piece. Fit one block at a time, using the spacing piece as a gauge to set the correct distance between them. Saw the ends off to form angles, as shown top right.

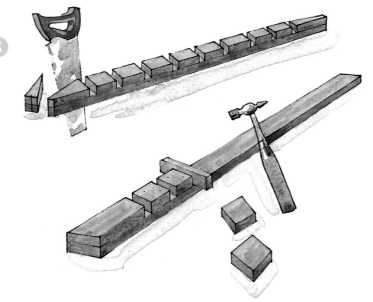

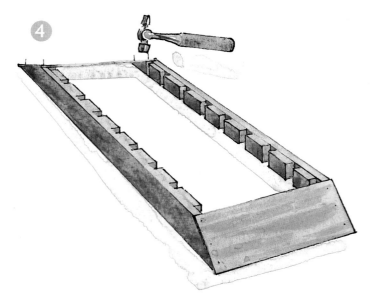

◄ The sawn, angled faces at either end of the uprights should be planed smooth. It is important that the uprights are set exactly parallel to one another and this can be done by placing a shelf in a slot at each end. A thin piece of card in the slots will prevent the final fit from being too tight. With a helper holding the assembly in this position, you can pin and glue the plywood panels onto the angled faces on the back of the bookcase.

TRADITIONAL BOOKCASE

This piece is designed to be made from solid wood. There are pine board products available from large hardware stores that are ideal for this project. Although any solid wood could be used, pine and pine moldings are conveniently prepared, and being soft, pine is relatively easy to work with. Follow the dimensions on the diagram, as the sizes are interdependent. The construction includes many of the techniques used in the preceding projects and you will need most of the tools mentioned so far. Finishing solid wood is in some ways easier than producing a good hand-painted finish. A finishing wax applied with a cloth is not susceptible to drips, runs, and brush marks as paint is, and will basically look as good as the surface of the wood. Although you will need to apply several coats, it is an easy task and far less messy than painting. While a wax finish is fine for this type of project, for a more durable surface you may choose to add a sealing coat of varnish. Onto the bare wood, brush a polyurethene varnish thinned to 70% varnish/30% turpentine. When the surface is dry, sand it smooth with very fine sandpaper and apply two or three coats of wax. To make the job easier, you can apply a sealing coat of varnish or wax to the case before the back and shelves are fitted.

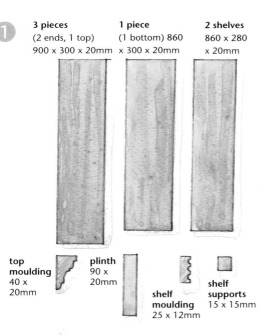

①

3 pieces
(2 ends, 1 top)
900 x 300 x 20mm

1 piece
(1 bottom) 860
x 300 x 20mm

2 shelves
860 x 280
x 20mm

top moulding
40 x 20mm

plinth
90 x 20mm

shelf moulding
25 x 12mm

shelf supports
15 x 15mm

▲ The ends of the wood boards for the top, ends, and shelves should be straight and square. Sand all faces of the boards now. The moldings can be bought by the length (you will need about 2 meters), and most stores have a range of styles to choose from. The overall dimensions of the sections should be broadly similar to those in the illustration. Leave the back slightly oversize for final planing after assembly.

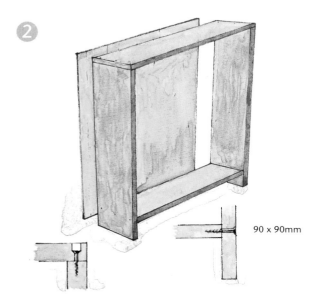

② 90 x 90mm

► The shelf supports should be 15mm square, and they should be as long as the width of the shelves. Screw them into place at the heights shown in the illustration on the right. Trim the wood for the plinth at the bottom of the case to length on a miter saw. Pin and glue these pieces. Leave the back ends of the side pieces and the ends of the front piece overlapping slightly for final planing when the glue has set. Make sure that the edges and front corner joint are properly aligned.

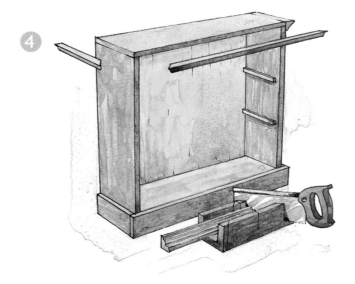

④

► Check that the shelves fit and if not, re-trim. Cut the moldings for the front edges of the shelves oversize, and pin and glue into place. Plane the tops and ends flush when the glue is dry. Glue the shelves into position, the lower one first. Put weights on each shelf to hold it down while the glue sets. Insert a screw into the middle of each shelf through the back of the bookcase to prevent them from sagging when

◄ Glue and screw the top and bottom butt joints together. Counter-bore the top holes to 10mm and use a corresponding plug cutter to make filling plugs. Hold the parts steady in a vise to mark the positions of the pilot holes. After assembly, wipe off excess glue with a damp cloth. Sand the areas around the joints when the glue has set and plane the top joint ends and all front edges flush. Pin and glue the back in place and plane the edges flush.

③

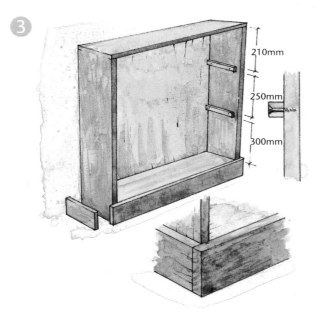

210mm

250mm

300mm

◄ The top molding is made up of three pieces mitered to form the corner joints. You can cut these using a miter box and a tenon saw (as shown left), or a miter saw (which is more accurate). Fit one of the side moulding pieces to the side of the case so that the mitred edge aligns with the front of the bookcase. Leave the back end of the molding overlength to be trimmed later. Pin and glue into place. Fitting the front molding is the most critical task as it is mitered on either end and there is no margin for error. Do this next. Then cut and fit the last piece of side molding. Trim the ends at the back flush and plane the top edge flat.

⑤

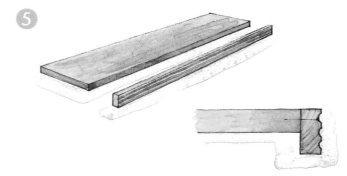

INDEX

AUTHOR'S ACKNOWLEDGMENTS

This book has been the work of a team and I would like to thank everyone who has contributed to it, particularly Alison Starling, Elisabeth Faber, Jo Walton and Martin Lovelock, and my wife Susanna.

The publisher would like to thank the following for their kind permission to reproduce photographs for use in this book.

KEY

b bottom, **t** top, **l** left, **r** right, **c** centre
OPG Octopus Publishing Group Ltd
CP Camera Press
BAL Bridgeman Art Library
EWA Elizabeth Whiting Associates
IA The Interior Archive
V&A Victoria and Albert Museum, London

Front cover Arcaid/Richard Bryant/Gale & Prior; **Back cover, l** Axiom Photographic Agency/James Morris, **r** EWA; **Back flap** Hanya Chlala

Endpapers Richard Davies; **1** IA/Henry Wilson; **2–3** Axiom Photographic Agency/James Morris/Architect Pip Horn; **5** IA /Fritz von der Schulenburg; **6 l** BAL/Biblioteca Medicea-Laurenziana, Florence; **6–7** AKG, London; **7 r** AKG, London; **8 l** AKG, London /Historisches Museum der Stadt Wien; **8–9 t** BAL/Private Collection; **9 b** AKG, London/Oskar Reinhart Collection, Winterthur; **10–11** IA/Fritz von der Schulenburg; **12** IA/Fritz von der Schulenburg; **13** Arcaid/Alberto Piovano/1993/Architect: Rosanna Monzini; **14 t** Lars Hallen/Design Press, **b** CP; **15** Richard Glover/Architect: John Pawson; **16** IA/C Simon Sykes; **17 t** CP, **b** CP; **18–19** International Interiors/Paul Ryan; **20** IA/C Simon Sykes; **20–21** Paul Rocheleau/ Bloedel House, Williamstown, MA; **21** IA/Fritz von der Schulenburg; **22 t** International Interiors/Paul Ryan/Skokloster Castle, **b** IA /Fritz von der Schulenburg /Alvar Aalto; **22–23** CP; **24 t** IA/C Simon Sykes, **b** Arcaid/Architect: Michael Wilford & Partners, Tate Gallery, Liverpool/ Richard Bryant; **25 t** Andrea Marks PR/Books etc., **b** IA/C Simon Sykes; **26–27** CP; **28** Robert Harding Picture Library/Jan Baldwin/Homes & Gardens/© IPC Magazines; **28–29** EWA; **30** Mainstream/Ray Main; **30–31** International Interiors/Paul Ryan /Victoria Hagan; **32** Arcaid/ Dennis Gilbert/Architect: Allford Hall Monaghan Morris; **32–33** EWA; **34 l** Arcaid/Alberto Piocano/1991/Designer: N Coombe, **r** Richard Davies; **35** Arcaid/John Edward Linden/Nick Butcher /Christian Davies; **36–37** Richard Davies; **38 t** EWA, **b** CP; **39** EWA; **40** IA /Jakob Wastberg; **41** EWA; **42** Michael Freeman/Kohiyama House, 1995/Yoyogi, Japan; **43** EWA; **44 l** Imaginazione Fornasetti, **t r** Tim Street Porter, **b r** Imaginazione Fornasetti; **45 t** IA/C Simon Sykes, **b** Abode; **46–47** Arcaid/Nicholas Kane/Original design by Maxwell Fry, remodelled by Robert Sakula and Cany Ash, 1995; **48** International Interiors/Paul Ryan/Architects: MC2 Design; **49** IA/Simon Upton; **50** Arcaid/Richard Bryant/Architect: David Wild;

51 Houses & Interiors/Mark Bolton; **52 t** Stocker Associates, **b** John Donat; **53** Vitsoe/Ken Kirkwood; **54** Axiom Photographic Agency/James Morris/ Architect: Pip Horne; **55 t** View/Peter Cook, **b** Arcaid/Alberto Piovano/ Architect: Mariano Boggia; **56–57** View/Architect: Cowper & Griffiths/Peter Cook; **58 t** Lars Hallen/Design Press/Dorfelt, **b** EWA; **59** Lars Hallen/Design Press/Dorfelt; **60 b** Arcaid/Jeremy Cockayne/ Architect: Andrew Yeats/ECO ARC whisky barrel house; **60–61 t** CP; **61** Abode; **62 t** EWA, **b** EWA; **63** CP; **64 l** EWA; **64–65** Marianne Majerus/ Design: Alistair Howe; **66** Arcaid/Dennis Gilbert/Architect: Bill Dunster; **67 t** IA/Wayne Vincent, **b** Arcaid/Nicholas Kane/Original design by Maxwell Fry, remodelled by Robert Sakula and Cany Ash, 1995; **68 l** University of East Anglia/Mr Jonathan Pritchard; **68–69** Gitta Gschwendtner; **69 r** Vincent Jalet; **70–71** Arcaid/Alan Weintraub; **72** Arcaid/Richard Bryant/Architect: Richard Rogers Partnership; **73** Michael Freeman/Charles and Ray Eames; **74** National Trust Photographic Library/Dennis Gilbert; **74–75** Paul Rocheleau/20th Century Architects; **76–77** IA/Simon Brown; **78** Arcaid/ Richard Bryant/Gale and Prior; **79** Ron Arad Associates/Christoph Kicherer; **80** IA/Andrew Wood; **81 t** Michael Freeman/Owings House/Jacona, **b** IA/Tim Beddow; **82** The Times/Jan Baldwin/Stocker Associates; **83 t** CP, **b** IA/Fritz von der Schulenburg; **84** Arcaid/Earl Carter/Architect: Greg Anderson; **85** Jerome Darblay; **86** IA/Jakob Wasteberg; **87** The Condé Nast Publications Ltd/House and Garden, April 1997/Simon Upton; **88** CP; **89 t** CP, **b** CP; **90 l** IA/Andrew Wood, **r** Mitchell Beazley/James Merrell; **91** IA/C Simon Sykes; **92** CP; **93 l** CP, **r** CP; **94 l** Crafts Council/Ron King, **r** Crafts Council/Roger Powell; **95 t** Crafts Council/Ron King, **c** Crafts Council/Romilly Saumarez-Smith, **b** Crafts Council/Les Bicknell; **96–97** View/Peter Cook/Tugman Partnership; **98** Marianne Majerus/Design: Barbara Weiss; **98–99** International Interiors/Paul Ryan/Kastrup & Sjunnesson; **99** EWA; **100 t** View/Conran Tugman/Peter Cook, **b** IA/Henry Wilson; **101** EWA; **102** Arcaid/Alberto Piovano/1991/Designer: P Robbrecht; **103 t** CP, **b** CP; **104 t** EWA, **b** Marianne Majerus/Design: Barbara Weiss; **105** Marianne Majerus/Design Barbara Weiss; **106–107** Robert Harding Picture Library Syndications/ Country Homes & Interiors/IPC Magazines Ltd; **108 b** Ralph Ball; **109 t** Ralph Ball, **b** Ralph Ball; **110–111** View/Greenberg & Hawkes/Peter Cook; **112** Henry Wilson/Mark Guard & Associates; **113 t** EWA, **b** Michael Freeman; **114 t** Arcaid/Richard Bryant/Architect: Richard Rogers Partnership, **b** National Trust Photographic Library/Dennis Gilbert; **115** View/Peter Cook /Architecton; **116** EWA; **116–117** Tim Street Porter; **117** Robert Harding Picture Library/David Giles/Homes & Ideas/© IPC Magazines; **118–119** IA/Fritz von der Schulenburg; **120** IA/Simon Upton; **121 l** IA/C Simon Sykes; **121 r** OPG/Simon Upton, **122 t** OPG/Enid Marx, **b l** AKG, London, **b r** V&A; **123 t** V&A/Eric Gill, **b** OPG/Faber & Faber/ V&A/Berthold Wolpe; **124–125** IA/Fritz von der Schulenburg; **126** National Trust Photographic Library/Nadia MacKenzie; **127** Arcaid/Richard Bryant/1987; **141** Michael Freeman; **142** View/Peter Cook; **143** EWA
For pp.**129–138** line artwork ©OPG/by Mark Ripley, colour artwork ©OPG/by Amanda Patton